1980

THE ENGLISH GYPSY
CARAVAN

Reading waggon by Dunton 1919

THE ENGLISH GYPSY CARAVAN

Its Origins, Builders, Technology
and Conservation

C. H. WARD-JACKSON
and
DENIS E. HARVEY

Drawings by Denis E. Harvey

DRAKE PUBLISHERS INC   NEW YORK

ISBN 0-87749-353-7

Library of Congress Catalog Card No 72-7313

Published in 1973 by
Drake Publishers Inc
381 Park Avenue South
New York, N.Y. 10016

Printed in Great Britain

CONTENTS

LIST OF ILLUSTRATIONS

LIST OF ILLUSTRATIONS

LINE DRAWINGS

SCALE DRAWINGS

CHAPTER ONE

THE TRAVELLING PEOPLE

Horse-drawn living waggons have been in use for at least a hundred and fifty years, and the best were built in Victorian England, notably in the last quarter of the nineteenth century and the first few years of the twentieth. The level of prosperity in Britain was then such that her travelling people could afford to live better than those of most countries. They may themselves mostly have been poor but they lived in a rich and vigorous society, and the itinerants of few other countries had the means of providing themselves with such good homes. By the 1890s these waggons had achieved a character at once distinctive, functional and handsome, so much so that they had already inspired recreational caravanning by the settled population.

The people of the roads themselves called their home their waggon, van or *vardo,* but house-dwellers called it a Gypsy caravan. For the Gypsies it was their most valued possession, so well-known that it would still be hard to find a better symbol of the travelling people. The term came into being and remained so because all the travellers were, to the settled population, Gypsies. That they may have had no Romany ancestry, that they may have been fair-ground folk, pedlars, tinkers or what have you, was not readily apparent. As they passed by, all that was clear was that their abode was not fixed, that they lived in vans, that they dressed outlandishly, that their complexions were dark. Even today, as one young *Romani-chal* said, 'If you're on the move you're a Gypsy—if you're settled you're just like everyone else'.

The kind of waggon called a Gypsy caravan is something more than one lived in by Gypsies. One would hardly use the term today of a motor trailer, whoever its occupants, but would normally imply by it a distinct kind of horse-drawn conveyance. We define it as the Gypsy caravan, regardless of whether it is or was the home of a Gypsy family; it could have been owned and used by other people, and many were and are. We exclude the heavy kinds of living waggon that well-to-do showmen and tourists often had built for them, sometimes pulled by traction engine. They do not have the characteristics common to the so-called Gypsy caravan, which is chimneyed, painted, one-roomed, four-wheeled, with door and movable steps in front (or back in only one type), a rack and pan-box at the rear, and an interior of more or less set plan, the whole sufficiently light in weight to be drawn normally by one horse.

Despite the fact that sixty years ago there were many hundreds of these on the roads of the British Isles, that the best of them exemplified craftsmanship and folk art of a high order, and that examples are conserved in and sought after by museums, no book of any kind has hitherto been available on them. The task of trying to fill the need has involved us in touring some obscure and unmapped byways of a varied kind, byways of practical day-to-day living, of history, rural technology, art and design, even philology. It has forced us to commit ourselves, for better or worse, to words and spellings in a subject verbally confused. A simple example: the Gypsy Lore Society, founded in 1888, spells 'Gypsy' with a 'y' (the word being an abbreviation of 'Egyptian'); and with a capital 'G' (it being the given name of a race though not the one the

12

people use in their own language, which is *Roma*). Yet in law the term refers to one following a particular way of life and not of particular racial origin, three learned judges having ruled to that effect. In this book we shall follow the spelling of the Gypsy Lore Society but use the word in its legal sense, differentiating people truly of the race as true Gypsies or Romanies, George Borrow's anglicised word.

Generally, the people of the roads, including Gypsies, true and otherwise, are today increasingly referred to by their own preferred soubriquet, the travellers or the travelling people. For reasons both good and bad, travellers have always excited controversy, an extraordinary fusion of suspicion, prejudice and even hatred, leavened with an often sentimental and romantic admiration that has clouded rather than aided understanding. Theirs is an image that is, in short, confused. Yet it is from their way of living that house-dwellers have derived one of their most widely followed recreations.

Caravans generally arouse in many a censure that is often reflected in laws and regulations that are unfair. Consequently the motorist who trails a van and carefully nurses public respect cannot always be relied on to welcome the thought that it was from the horse-drawn *vardo* that today's multiplicity of trailers derived. He may prefer his recreation to be unrelated historically to anything bearing the name 'Gypsy' with its age-long stigma. Nevertheless, recreational caravanning by horse and motor derived directly from what is known as the Gypsy caravan, an ancestry deserving of pride rather than shame, especially now that age has bred some veneration for it.

A hundred years ago houses-on-wheels were peculiar, not to the Romanies, but certainly to the travellers among whom they are numbered. Today they are used by all classes and kinds of people. There are believed to be well over 250,000 caravans in the British Isles. In 1970 nearly 60,000 trailer

13

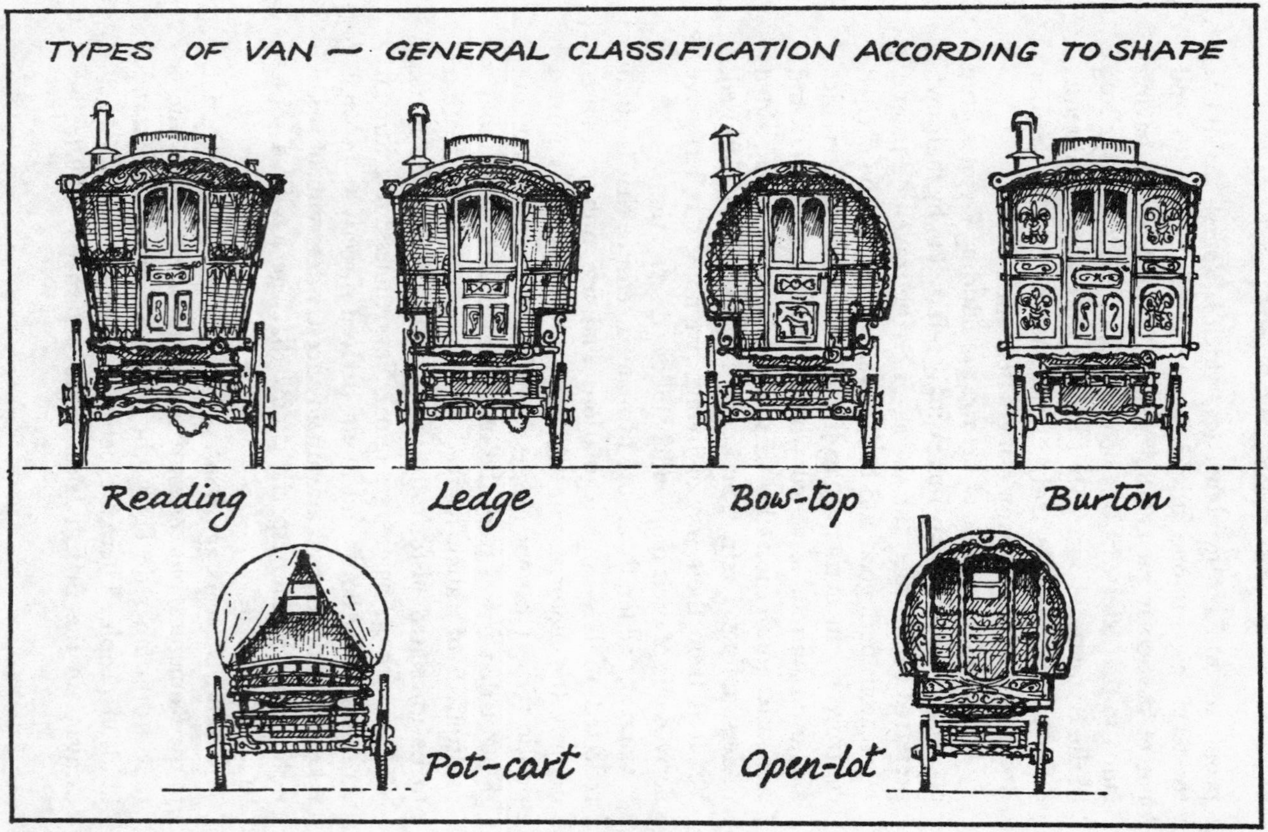

TYPES OF VAN — GENERAL CLASSIFICATION ACCORDING TO SHAPE

Reading   Ledge   Bow-top   Burton

Pot-cart   Open-lot

Fig 1

vans were made in Britain, twice as many as in France, the second largest European builder. One in six British families who go on holiday spend at least a part of it in a caravan and some 85,000 families live in mobile homes permanently. Additionally, in 1970 5,500 people bought motor caravans, as distinct from trailers.

Yet of the horse-drawn houses-on-wheels that aroused this passion for domestic mobility, fulfilled through the internal combustion engine and fed by an enterprising industry, little has been said and even less understood. Thanks to a Gypsy flair for verisimilitude when engaging the *gaujo*, or gorgio, non-Gypsy, fallacies about them abound. We have met people who really believe that there are 365 boards in the body of a *vardo*, representing the days of the year; that secret hiding places built into the interior were customary; that the best vans were each gilded with leaf from 100 special books imported from Germany. The printed word has perpetuated the belief that Gypsies covered Bow-top waggons with varnished otter skins, and that others insisted on the lintel over the door being made of unseasoned ash wood to ensure the fertility of the womenfolk within. Lintels are in fact of ash but for the less dramatic purpose of structural strength.

The museum visitor admiring the carving on an old Reading waggon, the owner of a Bow-top that stands in his paddock, or the photographer quick to capture the form and hues of an Open-lot drawn up beside the road, can understand little of the subject before him without some basic knowledge of the travelling people, past and present, for whom it was built.

WHO ARE THE TRAVELLERS?

A major difficulty in considering and understanding the travelling people, and their attitudes towards others, lies in answering the simple question: Who are they? House-dwellers differentiate between them merely as true Gypsies ('good') and others ('bad'), perhaps adding the afterthought, 'And there are those fair-ground people, or are they the same?' This sort of generalisation stems, like others, from ignorance, for the means of telling one class of traveller from another superficially is minimal. But the people themselves recognise a social structure of sorts.

The most respected class is made up of those families known to be of purest Romany blood. Their numbers today must be few, though it has been only in the last hundred years that intermarriage has thinned them. No doubt a large proportion of travellers do have some Romany blood, but to what extent is very problematic. People having no known Romany forebears at all who have adopted and followed Gypsy ways, often for generations, are known as mumpers, an old low slang word originally meaning beggar; with tinkers they are rated lowest in the scale, a scale now tending to be based rather more on possessions and less on origins. Then the people who are half Romany and half mumper are, in Romani, *poshrats* (literally 'half-bloods'). Others of mixed blood but less than half Romany are *didikais*, a word often used also in a loose sense as meaning 'not real Romany'. With a secret language of their own, Shelta, the tinkers are yet another class, believed by some to be descendants of Irish dispossessed landowners. For generations they lived nomadic-ally, surviving—until mass production—by working in tin, fashioning it into simple utensils, repairing kettles, pans and such. In Ireland many have been settled by the Dublin government, but about 600 families still live there under the most degraded conditions. Over the years the tinkers have crossed and re-crossed the Irish Sea.

The Gypsies, then, like the British people themselves, are by origin complex, and unified only by their way of life. The

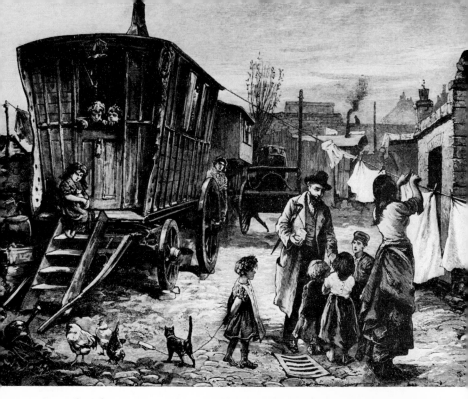

Page 17 (above) Engraving published 1879 of a Gypsy pitch at Notting Hill, near London, with an early Reading waggon; (below) gypsies and their waggons at Horsmonden, Kent, hop-picking 1949

Page 18 (above) The first pleasure caravan being pulled off soft ground by Durham miners, early 1880s; *(below)* a family on the road in Kent 1949 with a colt 'under training'

Gypsy Council today affirms 'the essential unity of the travelling people, above distinctions of group and origin'.

The main body of knowledge regarding the race has been built up painstakingly over many years by members of the Gypsy Lore Society, the volumes of whose journal are a repository of world-wide information. A member of its council, Stuart Mann, in his article in the *Encyclopaedia Britannica*, says *inter alia*:

> The living conditions of Gypsies are dictated by climate, geography and, above all, by the economic status of the host country, to which their own is invariably inferior. They are wealthiest in Sweden, poorest in the Balkans and southern Spain. Whatever their habitation, it is always in a sheltered spot, a sandpit, a quarry, a valley or a wood, away from the wind. British, French and German Gypsies live in painted caravans used mainly as sleeping quarters. Central European Gypsies build one-room brick cottages in sandpits or on wasteland. Farther east and in the Balkans their dwellings are of wattle and daub or other crude materials... Spanish Gypsies build their houses partly on the hillside... Coastal wanderers of Spain live in the sandstone caves...
>
> Gypsies profess the dominant local religion. Some of their poetry is original and chanted, but their dances, music, folk tales and proverbs are of local origin. Quarrelsome, quick to anger or laughter, they are unthinkingly, but not deliberately, cruel. Loving bright colours, they are ostentatious and boastful... They have little idea of time, proportion or measurement and are superstitious about childbirth, fertility, food and sickness. Their tribal customs sometimes have the force of law. Believing in charms and curses, they admit the falsity of their fortune telling. They betray little shame, curiosity, surprise or grief and show no solidarity...

Society, says Mr Mann, has always found the Romanies an ethnic puzzle and has tried ceaselessly to fit them, by force or fraud, piety or policy, coaxing or cruelty, into some framework of its own conception, but so far without success.

They have been nomadic for over a thousand years; and

their language, Romani, being related to those of north-west India, is the principal evidence for the belief that they originated from there, migrating first to Persia possibly well before the tenth century. Today there are perhaps two or three millions throughout the world, more than half in Europe. In Britain Appleby New Fair in Westmorland is their main annual concourse when, still, as many as a thousand horses change hands. The best Romani in Britain has survived in North Wales, and the language has given English a number of words, including *pal* and *cosh*. Anglo-Romani is now little more than a jargon, but today's Indian immigrants were not the first to bring Sanskrit words to the lanes of Britain, where they have been spoken for five hundred years.

The Gypsies reached Britain certainly earlier than 1500, and records show that at least the Scots welcomed them, yet many people came to fear them and from 1535 to 1783 repressive laws were passed that persecuted them unremittingly in a way that few other minorities have been. Believed by themselves to have come from Egypt, they were first called the people of Little Egypt, the Egyptians, then Gypsies. From 1635 dates the secondary usage of *Gypsy*—a cunning rogue. They were suspected and accused of the most nefarious behaviour, for example of stealing children, bleeding them to death and selling the bodies to anatomists. In fact, though they have a record of petty offence, it is one almost totally free of major crime. It was not until the mid-nineteenth century that George Borrow's books began a slow change in attitudes towards them.

In the European languages the equivalent words to *Gypsy* mostly resemble the Persian *zingar*—a saddler; and the Romanies' occupations have usually been either closely related to horses or to entertainment by musical or physical performance, with their womenfolk universally noted for fortune-telling. Their crafts of peg- and basket-making, chair-mending, flower-making, are believed to have derived from an early skill in wood-carving. They follow occupations often despised or not considered worth while by the settled population and, although economic pressures have caused abandonment of age-long ways of earning a living, it has usually been in favour of others related to the roads and the countryside.

The Gypsies have no written history or literature. Illiteracy has been imposed by their always being on the move, forcibly or otherwise, so that their children cannot attend school or only spasmodically. Of recent years the extent of illiteracy has been considerably reduced, yet among them formal education is not highly rated, and well after the universal education acts it was not unusual to refuse even to enter into relations with 'any chaps what knows how to write and count proper'. Illiteracy may then have been partly compensated for by the Romanies' remarkable inherited knowledge of country-living, skill with animals and herbal medicines. But the balance since has tipped heavily in favour of the classroom. Today young people either settle on sites or in houses or want the advantages only possible to the settled life.

Until about the third quarter of the nineteenth century taboos were numerous, mainly concerning women, death and food, and customs were observed rigidly. Choice of a marital partner was often limited not merely to the race but to the tribe; and marriage by the witnessed joining of hands was strong enough to be upheld in British courts. Rules to do with sex were strict, and beliefs often vaguely Oriental. The Romany custom best-known is, of course, the ritual burning of the belongings of the deceased.

All custom and taboo have been increasingly weakened since the 1870s by the influx of non-Romany blood, by the growth of cities and towns, by war service and the eclipse of horse transport by the petrol engine. The last enforced changes in occupation as well as in abode, though many find it difficult to adapt to indoor work in summer especially, during which backs are turned on sites and houses and the family is on the move.

The old ways die hard. We are reminded of a family of West Country travellers who live in an old Bow-top waggon permanently mounted on a motor-lorry, and a Midlander who has taken down a wall of his house and moved his *vardo* into the parlour so that he may live in it unmolested by the law. A century ago Borrow did not believe the Romanies could survive much longer. He was wrong. They change but remain.

TODAY'S GYPSIES

The first Government sociological study in Britain of Gypsies and other travellers was undertaken in 1965. It included such people living in caravans, huts and tents in England and Wales. It said:

Usually these people were isolated from the settled community. Although called travellers, some never moved from their base camp. They usually made a living by dealing in scrap metal, cars and other commodities, seasonal agricultural work, log and fire-wood cutting, casual labouring, hawking and begging, and rarely took a regular job. Travellers living on sites already established for them by local authorities were included. Excluded from the survey were those caravan dwellers on residential sites who were typically members of the local settled community, had regular jobs, and perhaps lived in caravans only because of the housing shortage. Also excluded were those families living in permanent shack and bungalow settlements who were essentially not travellers but part of the settled community... Others who were excluded were people of travelling stock now living in houses... tramps, showmen and circus people who were part of an organised group moving together, and families living on boats.

Previous estimates of the size of the Gypsy population varied from 20,000 'true Gypsies' in 1901 to 100,000 'travellers' today. The 1965 survey found that the traveller population of England and Wales numbered *at least* 15,000 persons in 3,400 'households', the majority in the south. Three quarters of them had never lived in a house and had always followed a nomadic way of life. Only six per cent now travelled by horse-drawn waggon, more common in the north than in the south. The great majority lived in trailers, providing more space than the traditional waggon. Their most serious problem was the constant search for a site where they could legally stop. The idealised notion of the free traditional Gypsy way of life was found to be far removed from present day reality, a life lived within a hostile settled society affording little opportunity of achieving acceptable living standards.

The traditional craft occupations were carried on by only a negligible proportion of males, the older rather than the younger. As many as half of all males were dealers, the great majority in scrap metal. Less than seven per cent were retired or unemployed. Three-quarters of all women were reported as not earning a living, with hawking the principal occupation of the earners.

Little evidence was found of any general wish by the settled population to improve the living conditions of the travellers, to free them from the injustice of being constantly moved on, to raise them from the position of a despised and isolated minority, or to educate their children. Equally it was clear that it would not be easy to break down the travellers' mistrust of the settled population, the result of ill-will experienced over many generations.

In 1968 Parliament passed an act making the provision of sites a duty of local authorities (the Netherlands had made such a law fifty years earlier!). The response was tardy. Nevertheless, plans are expected eventually to provide a legal place to live for about half of the known minimum Gypsy population, and the Gypsy Council themselves issued a code of good conduct for travellers in an endeavour to meet criticism of their ways. Yet these reforms have had a mixed reception even among travellers, some of whom fear assimilation. It is not surprising that Gypsies have recently sought to become nationalistic and organised. At a World Romani Congress held in 1971—the first since 1935, attended by delegates from thirteen countries—it was emphasised that half a million of their people had died in German concentration camps.

The degree of success (or failure) achieved by the more humanitarian, Government approach to the travellers' problems depends upon the extent of understanding and tolerance that can be generated by Gypsies and others alike. Because he has remained so different for so long, the Gypsy has always been difficult to fit into national and local structures. Yet, well beyond his numbers and station, by his very difference he has left his mark on countryside and town. Even London has at least nine Gypsy street-names and two Romany. In the words of the survey, their world is 'complete in itself, rich in human feelings and relationships'. The best one-volume work on it is Brian Vesey-Fitzgerald's *Gypsies of Britain*.

THE TRAVELLING SHOWMEN

The word 'traveller' has been used in the special sense of Gypsy for over a hundred years and the people themselves, considering that 'Gypsy' has become derogatory long since, have encouraged people to call them the travellers. But by no means are all travellers Gypsies. Roughly though not absolutely they may be said to be people whose means of livelihood causes them to reside mainly on the roads rather than in buildings. They include a wide diversity of people—

many road, construction and forest workers, and itinerants who 'work' the fairs, markets, carnivals, race-meetings and other concourses that provide ready-made audiences for entertainers and vendors.

Specifically excluded from the Government survey of the 1960s were the showmen who move from place to place in organised groups; their permanent caravan site needs have for many years been provided for by the Showmen's Guild of Great Britain, of which most are members. Where in the past these travellers appeared to the settled community to be Gypsy, they were commonly so-classed, though not consciously emulating the Romanies and, indeed, denying connection of any kind with them.

No substantial proportion of Gypsies are today capable of being classified as showfolk, and showmen themselves declare their separateness from Gypsies in no uncertain terms. It is considered to be an old fallacy that many Gypsies join circuses, and 'Lord' George Sanger in his autobiography was one who played down this commonly supposed relationship:

Now, I want to correct here a very popular error—namely, the belief that in those early days the gipsies were showmen, and most of the showmen gipsies. Nothing could be further from the truth. The gipsies, it is true, went from fair to fair, but it was as horse-dealers, hawkers of baskets and tinware, workers of the lucky bag swindle, fortune-tellers, and owners of knife and snuff-box shies. The showmen proper always kept themselves apart from the gipsies, who invariably camped in a different spot to that occupied by the caravans. I do not think I ever saw genuine gipsies acting as showmen, though I have known them as proprietors of very large drinking and dancing booths.

Yet perhaps because Gypsies and showmen were itinerants and frequented much the same places; because the circus, traditionally the heart of the showman's business, was based on the horse; and perhaps because the Gypsy has a gift of picking up a living in any milieu, the two have a relationship historically. Indeed, some Continental historians claim that most circus folk stem from one of the four main branches of the Gypsy people, the Sinti. They point to dozens of little tenting shows in which everyone from ticket seller to last acrobat on the bill is pure Gypsy. The Bouglionis, noted French circus proprietors from whom (among others) Buffalo Bill descended, were at least part Gypsy in origin.

Vesey-Fitzgerald, while saying that the circus and Gypsy worlds are distinct in Britain, lists the following vocations in which he personally knew Gypsies who practised: Punch and Judy showman, skittle alley proprietor, marionettist, bareback circus rider, palmist, boxer and, of course, fortune-teller. In the bare-knuckle days especially, he adds, the Gypsy was a power in the British professional prize-ring, and various champions of England were Gypsy-born. The word 'showman' suggests a well-to-do, top-hatted, proprietorial figure but in fact it covers a wide range of people, small as well as impressive, and Gypsies in the past were among the lesser ranks of these in quantity, often in time ceasing to be known as Gypsies.

Gypsy and showman have drawn apart with the passing of time and changed conditions, but they both toured in what the settled population called the Gypsy caravan. The Showman's Guild itself was formed eighty years ago to fight the introduction of legislation against all van dwellers. Thomas Murphy in his history of the Guild, states the circumstances. Between 1884 and 1889 George Smith, MP, was active in promoting Bills relating to people whose business was migratory. Having succeeded in introducing legislation against canal boat people, he turned to caravan dwellers, and pressed the House of Commons 'to provide for the regulation of vans, vehicles and tents used as dwellings'. Each van was to be registered every three years after approval by an authority.

The Bill was finally rejected after five years of bitter controversy, during which the UK Showman and Van Dwellers' Protection Association was formed, later becoming the Showmen's Guild, in 1918 registered as a trade union.

Although the hey-day of the travelling show is long past and touring has declined with the rise of the permanent fair-ground and amusement park, today some two hundred fairs alone are still held each week in season throughout the country. As with the Gypsies, showfolk are, by tradition, reluctant to give up the travelling life. Among them there is still the old saying, 'once a traveller always a traveller'.

These, then, are the travellers, past and present, for whom what we know as the Gypsy caravan was evolved and built. Let us now look at something of the history of the living waggon itself.

CHAPTER TWO

ORIGIN AND EVOLUTION

Perhaps it was the eastern sound of the word caravan, reinforced by the belief that the Gypsies came from Egypt, that gave birth to the fallacy that they brought the living waggon with them. Its Romanesque characteristics, its baroque carving, ostensibly picked up on wanderings through Central Europe, lent colour to the idea. In fact, the house-on-wheels, with stove as well as bed, does not pre-date 1800 at the earliest and we can find no evidence that true Gypsies took to it till about the middle of the nineteenth century.

The living waggon probably originated in France. In the eighteenth century Britain's roads were among the worst in Europe; being on an island the British relied on water transport. But France had 15,000 miles of what were then first-class roads by 1760, and the ruthless impressment of labour to build and repair them was a prime cause of the French Revolution. Napoleon set up the biggest building programme ever, and between 1804 and 1812 spent roughly twice as much on roads as on fortifications. By 1810 people travelled from Paris to Milan in as little as ten days.

Living waggons were then at least in contemplation in France, and their heating had been made possible by Count Rumford (1753-1814) who had already designed 'small ovens for poor families' and 'a portable kitchen furnace'.

It is likely that the house-on-wheels was first used by travelling menagerie proprietors who built vans for conveying their wild beasts and had the means of pulling heavy loads over bad roads. Certainly one early enthusiast was the Venetian-born patriarch of the circus, Antoine Franconi (1738-1836), in turn wild beast tamer, toreador, horse-breaker, equestrian, circus proprietor, and in his day to Paris what Astley was to London. Late in a long life he amused himself by constructing his *voiture nomade*, containing dining room, bedroom and galley. No examples of such early waggons exist, and evidence of their beginnings is very thin. In Britain the earliest known picture is dated 1840.

During the seventeenth and eighteenth centuries, indeed through a large part of the nineteenth, *caravan*, derived from the Persian *karwan*, was used for vehicles designed for carrying servants and fare-paying passengers. Before the Turnpike Road Acts of 1730 to 1780 it took six strong horses to draw stage-coaches and stage-waggons over the appalling roads; and it was not until the work of the engineers Thomas Telford and John McAdam took effect in the 1820s that Britain's roads even became capable of allowing people of simple means to live on them in waggons.

The travelling people of those days sometimes journeyed in tilted carts, though more usually afoot, and lived in tents.

In *Lavengro* (1851) George Borrow described a Gypsy encampment in about 1815:

Beneath one of the largest trees, upon the grass, was a kind of low tent or booth, from the top of which a thin smoke was curling; beside it stood a couple of light carts, whilst two or three lean horses or ponies were cropping the herbage which was growing high. Wondering to whom this odd tent could belong, I advanced till I was close before it, when I found that it consisted of two tilts, like those of waggons, placed upon the ground and fronting each other, connected behind by a sail or large piece of canvas which was but partially drawn across the top; upon the ground, in the intervening space, was a fire, over which, supported by a kind of iron crowbar, hung a cauldron; my advance had been so noiseless as not to alarm the inmates, who consisted of a man and a woman, who sat apart, one on each side of the fire...

In this venue Jasper Petulengro's father offers a home to the boy Lavengro, enticing him with 'You should live in a tilted cart by yourself and say prayers to us night and morning'. From this it would seem that, although in about 1815 Romanies lived in tents, it was not unusual for them to sleep in tilt carts.

Walter Simson, who gathered his material for *A History of the Gipsies* in the 1840s, gets a little nearer to the living waggon when he says:

In no part of the world is the gipsy life more in accordance with the general idea that the gipsy is like Cain—a wanderer on the face of the earth—than in England; for there the covered cart and the little tent are the houses of the gipsy...

Borrow first mentions caravans in connection with a fairground, when Lavengro (in the 1820s) goes to what appears to be Greenwich, but by the word he probably meant mere conveyances for equipment and wild beasts: 'I reached in about three-quarters of an hour a kind of low dingy town in the neighbourhood of the river; the streets were swarming with people, and I concluded from the number of wild beast shows, caravans, gingerbread stalls and the like, that a fair was being held.'

Lavengro takes over from a tinker and says to him: 'As for a home, I suppose I can contrive to make a home of your tent and cart.' Later he meets an itinerant Welsh preacher and his wife who 'take up their abode in the cart beneath the old oaks down there by the stream... they never sleep beneath a roof unless the weather is severe.'

In *The Romany Rye* (1857), set in about 1825, the jockey

at Horncastle horse fair tells Lavengro how he lived with old Fulcher, the basket-maker, in his caravan, but it is questionable at least whether this had any stove. More significant, in this book, Ursula Herne says to Lavengro: 'We are not over-fond of *gorgios*, brother, and we hates basket-makers and folks that live in caravans.'

From these sources it seems that by the 1830s, while the true Gypsies kept to their tents and despised travellers who lived otherwise, it was not unusual for tinkers, basket-makers and such to sleep in tilt carts, by then four-wheeled; that the older two-wheeled potters' cart, supported in a horizontal position on props, could have first been used in this way— perhaps the first move away from tents; and that *caravan* had yet to be used as meaning living waggon.

In *Wild Wales* (1862), set some time in the 1850s, Borrow makes his first certain reference to a living waggon. Lavengro again meets Black Jack Bosvile, The Flaming Tinman, not a true Gypsy but a 'half-and-half', travelling pugilist:

> After walking about half an hour I saw a kind of wooden house on wheels drawn by two horses coming down the hill towards me. A short, black-looking fellow in brown-top boots, corduroy breeches, jockey coat and jockey cap, sat on the box, holding the reins in one hand and a long whip in the other. Beside him was a swarthy woman in a wild flaunting dress. Behind the box on the fore-part of the caravan peered two or three black children's heads. . .

As Bosvile's van needs to be described as 'a kind of wooden house' it would seem that by the 1850s they were not common and it is still not clear whether it was equipped with a stove.

However, ten years before the period of *Wild Wales* there were already chimneyed caravans on the roads. Charles Dickens described one in 1840 in *The Old Curiosity Shop*, in which he put the travelling wax-works show-lady, his Mrs

31

Jarley, in a living waggon complete with bed and stove, altogether a splendid affair:

> It was not a shabby, dingy, dusty cart, but a smart little house upon wheels, with white dimity curtains festooning the windows, and window-shutters of green picked out with panels of a staring red, in which happily-constructed colours the whole concern shone brilliant. Neither was it a poor caravan drawn by a single donkey or emaciated horse, for a pair of horses in pretty good condition were released from the shafts and grazing on the grouzy grass. Neither was it a gipsy caravan, for at the open door (graced with a bright brass knocker) sat a Christian lady, stout and comfortable to look upon, who wore a large bonnet trembling with bows. And that it was not an unprovided or destitute caravan was clear from this lady's occupation, which was the very pleasant and refreshing one of taking tea ... the steps being struck by George, and stowed under the carriage, away they went...
>
> When they had travelled slowly forward for some short distance, Nell ventured to steal a look around the caravan and observe it more closely. One half of it—the moiety in which the comfortable proprietress was then seated—was carpeted, and so partitioned off at the further end as to accommodate a sleeping-place, constructed after the fashion of a berth on board ship, which was shaded, like the little windows, with fair white curtains, and looked comfortable enough, though by what kind of gymnastic exercise the lady of the caravan ever contrived to get into it, was an unfathomable mystery.
>
> The other half served for a kitchen, and was fitted up with a stove whose small chimney passed through the roof. It held also a closet or larder, several chests, a great pitcher of water, and a few cooking utensils and articles of crockery...

Dickens differentiates between this chimneyed van and the lesser vehicles of other travellers, including Gypsies. Also it may be noted that both Mrs Jarley's and Jack Bosvile's vans needed to be drawn by two horses, not one as became the norm on the better roads of the second half of the cen-

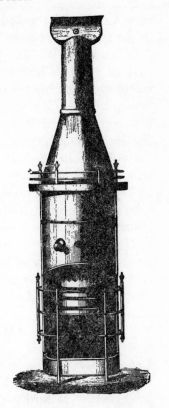

Fig 2 *The 'Colchester', brass waggon stove, colloquially 'The Policeman in the Corner'* (from an old catalogue)

tury. But otherwise Mrs Jarley's van is not unlike the later ones with which we are familiar. By the beginning of Victoria's reign, then, the kind of living waggon with which we are concerned was in use in England by showmen, although at that time a novelty.

The only consideration that puts this conclusion at risk is the two sketchy illustrations by Hablôt Knight Browne ('Phiz') accompanying the text. One shows the cottage-on-wheels with door at one side, the second shows a door on the other side. In so small a vehicle two side doors would render

33

practical layout almost impossible, and it is likely that the drawings were not done from actuality.

By the time of Mrs Jarley's van British roads had been macademised in increasing numbers and were the best in the world. Coaching was in its hey-day and coach-building boomed. The 1830s brought Shillibeer's first omnibus, the Hansom cab, and Robinson and Cook's brougham, named for the Lord Chancellor, its rigid body with elliptical springs and wheels attached, doing away with the old connecting pole or perch. Passenger-carriers had already been improved by being suspended on metal springs, and were called 'spring vans'. And just as *cabriolet* was reduced to *cab* so, from about this time, *caravan* began to be replaced by its abbreviation *van* for any common vehicle resembling a box with an arched roof, whether carrying people or goods. And *caravan* began to be used as meaning a waggon in which people actually lived.

THE SHOWMEN

Let us look a little more closely at the showmen of the time. Between 1821 and 1841 the population of the country increased by a third and its concentration in towns intensified. The fairs, the main places for centuries at which people bought and sold the things they could not provide themselves, consequently became less necessary for trading purposes as more people bought from shops. So more showmen became more concerned with fun and amusement and less with buying and selling. Curiosity, competition and movement had always been the essentials of their occupation, and some fairs became so boisterous and ill-behaved that the authorities closed them down. Showmen raced on narrow roads to get into the best positions on the *tober*, or site, often leading to fighting between the waggon trains. The show-

Page 35 (above) Vans at Little Egypt, Surrey, 1948; *(below)* modern Open-lot on a pitch in the Fens, 1970

Page 36 (above) Cavalcade of Bow-tops—Prices on the *drom* in Westmorland, about 1956. Note the 'siders'; *(below)* a well decorated modern Open-lot on the Great North Road, 1971

men's means of transportation thus became critical, especially with the application of steam to the merry-go-round or roundabout, which became the pivot of the fair-ground. All these influences directed their attention to the organisation of optimum utility from minimal weight and space.

Although the showmen prided themselves, and still do, on their separateness from even the best-born Romanies (who were equally disdainful of others), both classes of people had a close community of economic interests. Both were itinerant, both depended on and spent much of their time travelling between the great fairs, of which the traditional skills of the Gypsies were an integral part. To the showman horses and their well-being were vital, and few equalled the Gypsies as traders in horses, while they were farriers of ability. Also as fortune tellers their women were renowned. These interests alone sufficed to bring and keep the two classes together, yet each held the other very much at a social distance.

In addition to the showmen and the Romanies, who had their own language, customs and traditions, there were of course the lesser people of the *drom* on the move—the tinkers, basket-makers, brush-makers, half-and-halfs, *didikais*, broom-makers, potters, muggers, peg-makers, bagmen, chapmen, pedlars, the *hoi-polloi* of the highways. Some had Romany blood, most had none at all; but to the genteel, settled citizens all these wanderers, being of no fixed abode and otherwise lacking the badges of respectability, were all *Gypsy*. To the house-dweller caravans thus became Gypsy.

It was natural for the showmen to be the first travellers to live in waggons, just as it was for the true Gypsies to be the last. The showman had money and already employed the relatively heavy conveyances necessary for his equipment and wild beasts. And whether he was in a large or small way of business, he often built his waggons himself, probably on

37

drays made by cartwrights for the purpose or bought second-hand. By occupation he was adaptable, quick to sense change in taste, eager to modify his attractions to suit the public. But the Romany race was conservative and changed its ways only when it had to in order to live. Indeed, the well-born Gypsy prided himself on being Spartan and despised the comfortable, the fixed, the dependable, the material ways furthest from nature.

The early touring menagerists particularly had to pay special attention to the transport for their beasts, and they did not neglect their own comfort. A typical announcement by Polito's touring menagerie in 1805: 'During the Fair only.—The largest travelling collection in the known world, to be seen in six safe and commodious caravans, built for the purpose...' Another celebrated menagerie proprietor, who built his own waggons, was George Wombwell (1777-1850). In 1805 he began his 'caravan peregrinations throughout Britain', and built the waggons for his birds and beasts, including the giraffes. Many horses must have been needed to pull them.

Early attempts by showmen at building their own living waggons must have been very experimental. For instance, 'Lord' George Sanger (1827-1911) recorded that his father, invalided after Trafalgar from the Navy and turned peep-show proprietor and market trader, was 'in every way a handy man and soon got together materials for his first caravan' which 'had its roof and sides made of thin sheets of iron, and was far from comfortable. My mother has told me that in the summer it was baking hot and in the winter terribly cold, so that as a rule they preferred to camp in a tent, which they carried as part of the show.'

James Sanger possessed two horses only at this time, about 1820. He worked the fairs, village wakes and race-meetings in summer and traded between London and Newbury in winter, carrying provender from London for sale on his stall. By 1827, when George was born, his father had built another caravan and peep-show and in 1833, when George joined his parents on the road, his father had a waggon as well as a caravan. In the early 1840s the family caravan was about '12 feet long, just over 7 feet wide and about 7 feet high'. It could well have been built at Reading, only a few miles from Newbury, and may have been subsequent to one 'with gaily painted panels on which we looked with such innocent pride' that was thrown over by roughs 'with the side-door uppermost' enabling the family to escape from it.' At that time, said George, many persons looked upon van-dwellers and showmen as 'rogues and vagabonds' and it was common for them to be 'charged with the crime of sleeping out.'

When George Sanger retired in 1905 with a fortune of £30,000 after seventy years on the road he sold up everything but retained his living waggon. And in his last home 'his handsome bed bore another relic of his travels—a box rather like a lidless coffin. Being accustomed for so long to sleeping in a caravan, he could not rest unless there were boards for his elbow to knock against'.

THE RELUCTANT ROMANY

When did the true Gypsies, the Romanies, take to the *vardo*? Such evidence as there is suggests that it was little earlier than about 1850, after showmen had had living waggons of sorts in use for thirty years or more. Indeed, many clung exclusively to their bender tents till late in the century.

Old prints of Gypsies show them on foot, the women carrying babies, the men bundles, an ass or two with paniers on its flanks. The earliest engraving of a caravan with Gypsies that we have been able to find is dated 1879, the earliest photograph 1874.

Borrow finished writing his *Romano Lavo-Lil* in 1873 and in it he says 'The caravans are not numerous, and have only been used of late years by any of the English gypsy race.' However, his description confirms that by that time the conventional layout was established:

The caravan, called by the Gypsies *keir-vardo*, or waggon-house, is on four wheels, and is drawn by a horse or perhaps a couple of donkeys. It is about twelve feet long by six broad and six high. At the farther end are a couple of transverse berths, one above the other, like those in the cabin of a ship; and a little way from these is a curtain hanging by rings from an iron rod running across, which, when drawn, forms a partition. On either side is a small glazed window. The more remarkable object is a stove just inside the door, on the left hand, with a metal chimney which goes through the roof. This stove, the Gypsy term for which is *bo*, casts, when lighted, a great heat, and in some cases is made in a very handsome fashion. Some caravans have mirrors against the sides, and exhibit other indications of an aiming at luxury, though in general they are dirty squalid places, quite as much as or perhaps more than the tents, which seem to be the proper and congenial homes of the Gypsies.

To summarise, then, it seems reasonable to say that the people of the roads at first took the tilt or cover from their cart to sleep beneath, having too few or no tents; that they later slept beneath the tilt in the cart itself when conditions were unusually rough, a habit likely to have grown with the four-wheeled tilt waggons made possible by better roads; that in the first quarter of the century showmen, great and small, began to live on the road in waggons sometimes constructed by themselves; that travellers of other kinds with sufficient means copied this mode of living; and that somewhere around mid-century the Romanies began slowly to follow suit.

It could not have been long before it was found that country wheelwrights and wainwrights were best able to provide maximum living comfort for minimal cost, and craftsmen of this kind located in places well frequented by travellers came to specialise in building caravans. Some also may have been made by builders of fair-ground equipment, also becoming a specialised business. The types of van that each man built were limited only by the skills he commanded and his customers' requirements and pocket. Such work as he and his men could not do was done for him by other master-craftsmen in the vicinity or by journeymen.

Early vans must have been very varied in form, and pictures exist of some eccentric constructions that persisted into the second half of the century. But among people on continual move ideas were interchanged rapidly and improvements in layout introduced in one area soon became known to builders in others. Gradually, and probably by the 1850s, trial and error evolved the layout that became more or less standard. It was found, for example, that a frontal or possibly rear door, instead of one at the side as in Mrs Jarley's van or that recalled by George Sanger, was most economic of space.

Nevertheless, the vans reflected characteristics identified with their place of build, sometimes thence deriving the name by which they came to be known—the Reading, the Burton. One class of waggon, the Brush or Fen, was evolved to meet the trading as well as the living needs of travellers who made and hawked brooms, baskets and mats—the Broom Squires as they were sometimes called. But it is only in retrospect that the products of the builders can be resolved into the six types described in Chapter Four, three of them more closely identified with the Gypsies than the showmen.

The Gypsy-suited vans had the body slung *between* tall wheels with floors consequently narrower than others. These were best for crossing fords and for pulling off road onto rough ground. The other types all have wheels *under* the bodies and were found to be better suited to good roads, admitting a greater width of floor not possible with the Gypsy types unless their axles were extra long and the track of the waggon consequently inconveniently wide.

Small-space design ingenuity with its emphasis on inbuilt furniture, probably first seen in sea-going vessels, is common-place today and carried to its ultimate in motor-trailers, aircraft and space capsules. But over a century ago technology and materials were simple, and the space economy achieved in the old waggons exemplified outstandingly the designing ability of the men who built them with little more to go on but the precepts of the shipwrights. They had no pattern-book by a Chippendale or Sheraton, and ran modest little family firms with the simplest equipment, 'working by the eye and fairing up', without plan or drawing of any kind, the partners illiterate but with inherited craft skills.

By tradition Burton-on-Trent was the source of the type of waggon most used by showmen, and Reading of the type thought most highly of by Gypsies—for such notes as we have been able to gather on the builders there and at other places please refer to Chapter Five.

At least in the hey-day of the *vardo* the family most widely reputed as builders was Dunton of Reading, and it is prob-able that in the Reading waggon the Gypsy caravan reached its highest and most characteristic form. It was made at other places as well, of course, but did it originate from Reading in the first half of the century? We can only say that the circumstances of the place favoured that. Reading in 1846 with a population of 19,000, was at the centre of southern England, astride the Bath Road, the highway to the West-country; less than forty miles from London's wealth, and the principal southern resort of travellers of the time. The town shipped large quantities of timber down-Thames, was a canvas-making and barge-building centre, had six wheelwrights, seven harness-makers, and twenty-two corn merchants. By the 1870s it had seven coach-builders. What we know as the Reading type of van had certainly been evolved by the 1860s

Although one often sees advertisements offering Gypsy caravans over 100 years old, such enticements should be treated with reserve (see Chapter Nine). Few exist which predate 1900. They were not built of hard, century-lasting timbers, and almost all at one time or another have suffered rough treatment and neglect. Many over the years deteriorated into an appalling condition, were badly repainted if at all, became rotten and finally fell to pieces. Others were ritually burned with other possessions when their Gypsy owners died. The few that over a long period retained their condition and charm were in the hands of showmen or well-born Romany families who cared for them with the persistence, pride and skill of the most house-proud suburb dweller. They were their owners' primary possession when Gypsy-owned and were invariably returned at intervals to the *gaujo* builders, whose craftsmen repainted and reconditioned them. Much the same is true of the best survivors of the showmen's waggons, though this class of traveller often had as friends craftsmen who, normally employed on keeping equipment in condition, were available to refurbish the waggons.

The *vardo* became the Gypsy woman's most coveted possession, the paramount domestic status symbol. Rodney Smith, better known as 'Gipsy' Smith, the evangelist, was born in 1860 in a tent, the son of Gypsies. His autobiography records that in the spring of 1877 the family travelled from Cambridge to London in their waggons. He said:

> The young gipsy couple start their married life by purchasing a waggon. This costs anywhere from £40 to £150 and is obtained from a gorgio waggon-builder. Oddly enough, the

43

gipsies never learn the trade of making their own waggons. The waggons are very warm and very strong, and last a great many years. The young husband is, of course, the manufacturer of the goods, and his wife the seller. When she leaves the waggon in the morning to go her rounds she arranges with her husband where the waggon shall be placed at night, and thither she betakes herself when her day's toil is over. In the course of the day she may have walked from fifteen to twenty miles. If the husband has been refused permission to stand his waggon on the arranged spot and has had to move on, he lets his wife know where he is going by leaving behind him a track of grass.

We do not find it odd, as Smith says he did, that the Gypsies did not learn the trade of waggon-building. The crafts involved were more skilled perhaps than he appreciated, and their rudiments took some years to master; also builders would hardly be likely to accept Gypsies as apprentices. It demanded an investment in tools, timber and premises, and above all a settled, steady way of life—anathema to the Gypsy of those days.

PLEASURE CARAVANNING

In about 1880 eccentric, fresh-air-seeking gentlemen began to hire or buy caravans and holiday in them on the roads, though hardly for long when the conveyance was second-hand. 'I would as soon buy an old feather bed in the East End of London as an old caravan,' wrote one. 'There is a chance of guests in old caravans of the gipsy class that you would not care to be shipmates with.'

This man was William Gordon Stables, Scots surgeon and medical doctor, retired naval officer, bicycling enthusiast and boys' book author. He was the father of pleasure caravanning, and wrote a most engaging book about it, published in 1886, *Cruise of the Land Yacht 'Wanderer'*. His van cannot be classed under the heading of the subject of this book, and he travelled like a lord, but it is the link between the Gypsy caravan of the 1870s and the light-weight trailer and motorised vans that traverse the world today. It demonstrates how the old living waggons, with their baroque decorations so utterly unlike today's streamlining, came to exert a powerful influence on society generally.

Stables' van and his 1,300-mile tour in it, resulted from his going in a pony-trap one summer's day through the Thames-side village of Great Marlow where some vans were drawn up beside the road. Flying swings so startled his horse that she made 'a determined attempt to enter a draper's shop' and the damage done to the trap required him to stay over for repairs. While waiting he was invited by the owner into the prettiest of the caravans in which 'the space was limited owing to the extraordinary breadth of the bed and size of the stove'. He obtained from the owner the address of the builder, and wrote to him for an estimate for a waggon for himself. The reply he received read: 'Wich i can build you a wagon as ill cary you anyweres with 1 orse for eity pounds. I as built a power o' pretty wagons for gipsies, an' can refer you to lots on 'em for reference.'

Stables could afford something better and went to the Bristol Wagon Company, specialists in constructing Pullman cars for Britain and America. They built to his design the 'Wanderer', twice the length of a *vardo* and looking like an elegant cross between one and an American railroad car of the time (see plate page 18).

Of solid mahogany outside and lined with softer wood, it scaled 30 hundredweight at Bristol and, loaded up, under two tons—about twice the normal *vardo* weight. Loading-up included master, valet and coachman and a large Newfoundland dog! It was the valet's job to reconnoitre the road ahead on a tricycle and seek out overnight accommodation, for they put up at inns and stabled the horses. Coachman and valet slept in the inn, the master in his van in the yard! It is not surprising that Stables found one horse insufficient.

Stables, who differentiated between a pleasure-seeker—a *caravanist*—and a professional—a *caravanite*, gave advice as valid today as then: a caravan 12ft long serves every purpose, easily moved by one good horse; a gentleman-Gypsy's carriage should be unornamented and not 'resemble that of a travelling showman', yet not look like a Salvationist's 'barrow'; a single-horse van should not, loaded, be over 15cwt; study regularity and tidiness above all things—keep all 'as bright and clean as a new sovereign'; everything that can be done the evening before departure should be done; make an early start and all will go well; drink no water that has not been filtered—and so on.

One more quotation from this health enthusiast's book, still informative, amusing and readable—his description of a train of showmen and Gypsies met on the way to Falkirk fair:

> Here they come and there they go, all sorts and shapes and sizes, from the little barrel-shaped, canvas-covered Scotch affair, to the square yellow-painted lordly English van. Caravans filled with real darkies, basket caravans, shooting-gallery caravans, music caravans, merry-go-round caravans, short caravans, long caravans, tall caravans, some decorated with paint and gold, some as dingy as smoke itself, and some mere carts covered with greasy sacking filled with bairns; a chaotic minglement of naked arms and legs, and dirty grimy faces; but all happy, all smiling, and all perspiring. Some of these caravans have doors at sides, some doors at front and back; but invariably there are either merry saucy children or half-dressed females leaning out and enjoying the fresh air. . .

Stables still uses *caravan* for vans not necessarily designed to live in; and it would seem that the train included grand showmen's waggons 'with doors at sides' more resembling Pullman coaches than anything and quite unlike what we know as Gypsy caravans. From the latter part of the century rich showmen had homes constructed that were miniature copies-on-wheels of elegant residences of the day, and had more in common with railway coaches built for Royalty than with the *vardo*. They were drawn by steam traction engines, and sometimes reached as much as thirty feet in length, weighing ten tons, equipped with electric light, and panelled in mahogany.

THE LATER NINETEENTH CENTURY

The *vardo*, always built to order, multiplied in the latter years of the century. More travellers now had more money than their fathers and grandfathers and a few could even be considered well-to-do. Between 1841 and 1901 the population of Great Britain more than doubled and in spite of the spread of the railways still moved about largely by horse. In the 1890s the horse count was reaching its zenith, and the fairground everywhere reached its peak of prosperity.

The Gypsy caravan became commonplace along with the bicycle. Families, whose ancestors had known nothing better than their tents, were of secondary account among their fellows if they did not travel in waggons, the best of them the high-wheeled Reading; the showmen, if not in the traction-engined coaches that were the prerogative of the few, in the lower-wheeled Burton. But there was no sharp dividing line between the one-horse vans of the showmen and those used by Gypsies. Vans were chopped and changed frequently, and a Romany family was almost as likely to live in one type as another. But to the stay-at-home house-dweller all these chimneyed vans were Gypsy. Many were very rough-and-ready, but the best were gold-leafed masterpieces of good-housekeeping, with fine silver-ware and porcelain, spotless linen, good featherbeds and eiderdowns, and shining stoves.

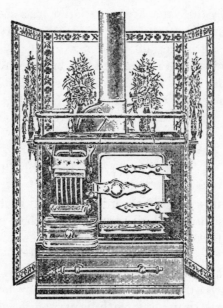

Fig 3 *The 'Hostess' stove* (from an old catalogue)

A sleeping place can easily be improvised, but not so a fire in a wooden vehicle. So the basic furnishing essential was the stove, and in the best vans its iron-work was kept black-leaded and armour-bright, its brasses buffed and brilliant. The hearth was no less the heart of the home of the traveller than of the house-dweller, yet the Gypsies used their stoves for cooking only when the weather made an outside fire inconvenient. Said Silvester Gordon Boswell in his autobiography:

In our waggon we had a stove that was well known in waggon time. But Mother used to cook outside in a Dutch oven, an eight-gallon cast iron boiler—and we could put a turkey in that, and put it over a stick fire, or next to a stick fire, and it would roast and roast and roast until it was absolutely brown and beautiful... I think most old-fashioned Gypsy people like us wouldn't be without a Dutch oven...

48

What were called American stoves came into common use in caravans from the 1860s. Free-standing, cast iron cooking stoves were first marketed in the USA around 1830, and soon their use was widespread. They were movable, did not require bricking in, were highly economic of fuel and were small relative to the Old Country's open fireplaces and grates built into the wall that sent most of the heat up the chimney (an English kitchen often squandered ten tons of coal a year!) The American stoves were soon copied.

Their principal populariser in the British Isles was James Smith, Edinburgh-born in 1816. He emigrated, became a metalworker and set up store in Jackson, Mississippi. He returned to Scotland with the American stove idea, and started selling them in Glasgow in 1856. One of his first was used by Florence Nightingale at Scutari in the Crimea. By 1857 he had founded Smith & Wellstood, Columbian Works, Bonnybridge, Scotland.

While Smith based his appeal on the principle of more heat for less fuel, the small size and ease of installation of his products rendered them suitable for sea-going vessels, and several of the smallest were found by caravan-dwellers to be just what they needed. The best-remembered nineteenth century caravan stove is the 'Colchester', succeeded in time by the 'Hostess' (Figs 2 and 3). They are described in Chapter Seven.

An improvement in van design probably introduced in the last quarter of the century was a kind of raised roof having clerestory windows along either side (Fig 4). It allowed greater headroom and provided toplight and ventilation. There were two kinds: the Pullman roof, running the full length of the top of the van, and derived from the sleeping car design (1867) of the American, George Mortimer Pullman; and the mollicroft, stopping short at the over-hang, front and back. Surviving Reading, Ledge and Burton waggons normally incorporate one or other pattern.

49

Some Typical
Mollicroft Skylights

Wright Ledge

Reading
and Ledge

Burton

Pullman type

Fig 4

Of the two the commoner is the mollicroft and is perhaps most characteristic. Why mollicroft? Possibly the originator lent his surname to it, and if so he otherwise remains anonymous. It may or may not be a coincidence that *molly* is nineteenth-century standard English for an effeminate person; while *croft* was often used as meaning a simple habitation. Thus, a mollicrofted van—one made for a molly-head, molly-mop or 'softie'. The first vans having these mollicoddling toplights could well have earned this kind of light-hearted jeer, especially from Gypsies.

The Gypsy caravan was born around the beginning of Victoria's reign and was in range of its eclipse at her death. In 1901 it showed no appearance of decline, for there were probably more on the roads in Edward VII's time than before or after; but in 1895 the first petrol-engined horseless-carriages were on the road ten years after Carl Benz had invented them, and that marked the beginning of the end of horse-drawn vehicles generally. In that year, too, the first public showing was given of the cinematograph by Lumière at Lyons, France, and that in time brought about the decline of the fair-ground and circus as the most popular public entertainment. Yet both events seemed then utterly remote from the *vardo*. After all the Fair was older than the road itself, and the Horse older than the Romanies. The caravans continued to roll.

More and more roads were hard surfaced, and pleasure caravanning attracted more people. At a meeting on 14 June 1907 of eleven enthusiasts the Caravan Club was formed for the ladies and gentlemen who had followed the example of Gordon Stables. By 1913 it had 300 members. Some had waggons specially designed for them, others were in the Gypsy style, and today the largest club of its kind in the world with over 70,000 member families retains its symbol of the horseshoe. But change was coming. Even then there were one or two motorised caravans on the road (Austin for one), though they were excessively heavy. And while in 1904 there were about 8,000 cars in the British Isles, there were 53,000 by 1910.

FROM 1914

Even so, in 1910 the automobile was still a novelty at which people stared, and moving pictures little more than 'extras' at the music-hall. Even when war was declared in 1914 people were still not used to the idea of the car, though they certainly were within four years. It was the omnibus that took troops to Flanders, the Paris taxis that carried the *poilus*. War demands forced car manufacturers into mass production, to which Henry Ford had shown the way in 1908 with his Model 'T', and by 1920 the internal combustion engine was fully established.

Thousands of horses shipped to all theatres of war had been killed. The equine population of Britain shrank, and with it the way of life of many people based on it. Now, as well as the motor-car, omnibus and taxi-cab, there came the commercial petrol-driven vehicles, evolved and multiplied to carry guns, munitions and supplies. In 1900 there were 40,000 horse-drawn omnibuses in London alone, plus 4,000 tram-horses, but by 1924 they had all gone, and the total horse population had dropped to less than two millions.

Between the wars the showmen were quick to adapt themselves to the fast-changing conditions of the amusement revolution. They had harnessed steam to their roundabouts and other equipment at an early date, and their traction engines puffed along the roads of the 1890s. After 1920 they turned over their pulling power from horse and steam to petrol and oil, and by the 1930s few travelled in their old Burton waggons. The Romanies still clung to their *vardoes*,

Page 53 Characteristically decorated interior of a Reading by
Dunton. Note the 'Angel' lamp at right

Page 54 (above) Reading by Dunton, 1909, with inter-rib carving and panel shutters; (below) another version of the Reading by the same builder, 1919

the economics of their lives probably complicated as never before by the contraction in horse-trading and the changes on the *drom*. By 1948 the national horse count was a mere 612,000, and very few of the old living van builders had survived the wars and depressions.

Yet, despite it all, the tradition of the *vardo* persists even into the 1970s, perpetuated not by holiday-makers or social drop-outs but by Gypsies themselves, some six per cent of whom still live in horse-drawn waggons. And between the wars a modern horse-drawn van came into being that can be fairly classified as a distinct and sixth type—a simplified affair that lends itself to standardisation of production: the Open-lot, sometimes called the Yorkshire Bow. They are still occasionally built, direct descendants of the tilted pot-cart, a glorious if infrequent sight on the roads and at horse fairs (see plates, pages 35 and 36).

So, while most travellers have gone over to trucks and trailers, and the sons of generations of horse-copers have picked up the trade of car mechanic or turned to making a living as scrap metal merchants from the discards of subtopia and the concrete jungle, there are even yet a few who whistle to the walking pace rhythm of the horse's hooves. The Romanies, the traditionalists, were the last to take to the chimneyed house-on-wheels. They are the last to leave it.

D

CHAPTER THREE

ON THE ROAD

The footboard of a moving, horse-drawn living waggon is one of the best seats in the world. You drive from the nearside, where you have control of the brake and can jump down easily to drive from the curb or go to the horse's head. Riding up you are snug in your corner, with your left arm hooked over the carved bracket beside you, your legs propped on the 'sharps', or swinging two feet above the road. The reins are slack in your hands, and a fine mare pulls steadily as though hynotised by the rhythm of her own hoofs. There's the gentle rumble and swing of the waggon behind you, the clink and rattle of the bit and harness links, sometimes a low voice singing—and, ahead, the road. It is not quite the winding, white road of the romantics, but a dirty grey or brown. Yet, like life when you're young, it stretches ahead, beckoning through the countryside.

In the British Isles the landscape often changes completely within a few miles. Towns and villages are only a short distance apart, and their people are still very much a part of the place in which they live—that is, when your pace allows you to get to know them. A change of environment can be enjoyed in much less than three hundred miles at 60mph. In under twenty miles, a day's travel, the Gypsy—his people, home and all he possesses—emigrates to a new land.

One of the Smith waggons we once travelled with pulled up at a roadside cafe. A man there seemed to think the horse-drawn van was an obsolete mode of conveyance. When he heard Smith was heading for Kent and would take two days he smiled.

'I'll be there in two hours,' he said.

'I'm sure you will,' said Smith, equally scornful, 'but you'll have to come all the way back again, won't you?' He spat between the shafts. '*And* you'll be late for yer tea... I tell you something—bet you a fiver I get my house over to Kent afore you do.'

Most *gaujo* scoffing at a *vardo's* rate of travel derives from the fallacy that a Gypsy waggon is primarily a vehicle. It is not, it is a home. Its wheels are fundamental yet incidental to its purpose, much as foundations are fundamental yet incidental to a house. Like any home it is a base, but a mobile one. For communications and fast travel, a trap or flat-cart is used and can make spanking good time. Gypsies seldom need to take their van more than fifteen miles in a day, usually to the next good pitch along the road, an objective that scarcely calls for motor transport. As to the economics of it, we heard one traditionalist Cooper telling it straight to a car-minded *gaujo*: 'When they invents a motor what'll fill its own tank overnight like what this good little mare do, look, then I might think of choppin' for it.'

Reinforced by the common misconception that the Gypsy is pathologically lazy and irresponsible, another fallacy must be corrected. This one is spread by generations of children's story-tellers, in which Mum, Dad and their off-spring revel in a caravan holiday—a jolly six weeks of peaceful rolling from one village to another over level country roads with a dear, wise old horse between the shafts. In fact, the horse is never wise and, if old, hasn't the strength to do his job.

Anyone who has spent a single day on the road with a

living waggon will know that the responsibility of that alone is more than enough for the average *gaujo*. The surest way to court trouble is to rely on the good sense of the horse. Even the best of horses, though lovable, are often foolish. They can be taught some things but mostly are erratic and dim-witted, sometimes intuitive but seldom intelligent.

THE HORSE

An ancient notebook, written for the guidance of young cavalry officers, began: 'In the cavalry there are two kinds of Management: Man Management and Horse Management. The most important of these is Horse Management.' This is as true for the van dweller. Manage the horse well, and the van will look after itself—or almost.

First-time travellers with a Gypsy van find the experience very different from their expectation, even within the first few yards if the ground is rough. After several refusals the horse starts off in a series of spasmodic, but seemingly gargantuan, leaps and plunges which snap the body about on its springs like a jack-in-the-box. This performance is accompanied by thuds and shocks from the interior and the crash of falling crockery, sounds that persist for some seconds after the driver has pulled up, if he is so able, on level road. When all is quiet and he climbs up on the footboard and looks in, he finds all he possesses in chaos on the floor.

'I sold a van to a gen'leman once,' one of the Smiths revealed, 'and I was downright sorry for 'im. Between you and us it warn't a very good one but de wheels was sound and he thought he'd go for a spin on the road wiv it. Well, he disremembered to untie de wireless aerial from up top of a tree by de van, look. When he pulled out, de wireless-set jump wack-up fru de sky window and took half de roof off. Quite spoilt his 'olidays.'

The right kind of horse is a heavy cob of about 14 hands, used to working in harness and in heavy traffic. He will have been accustomed to living waggons from the time he first set hoof on the road. To familiarise a colt to a waggon and motor traffic a Gypsy hitches him with a short rope from the head to the trace-ring on the collar of the shaft-horse, preferably his mother (see plate page 18). Thus led, he walks along on the offside, always under the eye of his owner. So apprenticed he learns, for example, that he does not stop halfway up a hill, where there is not enough grip on the polished surface to start from a stationary position. A Gypsy-trained horse pulls till he gets to the top, knowing from experience that he will enjoy a rest when he gets there.

One of the Dorset Coopers had a story that illustrates that confidence is at least half the need on bad hills. 'We was drivin' out one day down country when we comes up with a gen'leman with an 'orse and waggon. He was stopped halfway up a hill and couldn't get no further. The van was all loaded up with *gaujo* stuff, campin' stuff, and as we come up he was trying to get a big tin bath off of the cratch to lighten the load, look. Well it gets stuck, see, and as we come up, the whole cratch come away and all his *covvels* comes bouncin' down the hill past us.'

Cooper went on to say how he told 'the gen'leman' to stand away, refixed the cratch, loaded the bath and other things— his *covvels*—back onto it, spun the van around in the road and drove back to the bottom of the hill.

'I climbs up then and starts the mare up the hill at a run, my brothers, and got her up over the top before she even felt the waggon behind her.'

To help pull in hilly country a second horse, a 'sider', is often hitched alongside the shaft horse, the traces running back to a swingle-tree or 'spreader' linked to a ring-bolt on the underside of the off summer. A rope or strap goes from

Spreader attached to
offside summer

Fig 5

the sider's head to a ring on the collar of the shaft horse, the
driver having a single rein to the offside snaffle rings (see Fig
5 and plate page 36).

A horse used to farm work, however powerful, is not
qualified to pull a caravan. He can be schooled to work well
enough but that takes time and trouble. The unaccustomed,
tall overhang of a waggon front discourages some and
frightens others. A farm horse has no way of telling that a
vardo is hollow and, if he does not mistrust it on sight, he
probably takes it for a loaded farm waggon. Not usually
expected to pull such a load by himself he quickly loses heart
and jibs when the road mounts a hill.

The frightened horse is the worst. He may try to leave his
burden behind. We once saw an Irish mare of this kind in
the shafts. The sight of the waggon did not appear to worry
her, but then some twigs of a roadside sapling scraped the
waggon side, slapping each of the uprights in turn. She was
off at a gallop, the driver running with her. Had he been
riding up at the end of the reins he might have held her, or
at least kept her in the road till she tired; but there was no
time for him to get back. He managed to hold the road some
of the time and keep her headed straight but she kept kicking
his legs out from under him. She was trying, too, to keep
track of the waggon behind instead of the way ahead, and

when the road swung away to the right the Gypsy couldn't turn her. The old van was thundering along, and he was still swinging on the bit when they went slap through a hedge and overturned down a bank.

There are ways of staving off this kind of mishap when there is time to act. Controlling the horse from the footboard, at the reins' end, is the best. The old hat on the Gypsy's horse's head, beloved by the illustrators of children's books, probably had its origin in a strictly utilitarian purpose. It would be tied on to prevent a 'green' horse from seeing back over the top of his blinkers.

Once in a crisis on the road one of the Smiths asked for a pegknife, cut a piece out of a red and white striped tarpaulin over the cratch of his waggon and blindfolded the mare with it. Next he commandeered a green-and-yellow striped necktie from his son, cut it in half and used it to tie the bandage to the throat strap each side of he mare's head. To the wide-eyed puzzlement of *gaujos* as we passed, she pulled us several miles in this outlandish millinery.

Most Gypsy horses are unusually well-conditioned, due both to the care they receive and the varied diet of the commons and roadside verges. The owner of a well-known racehorse stud once told us that when one of his horses was convalescing he would follow the advice of a Romany acquaintance and peg it out by the roadside. The horse will instinctively select from the hedgerows the plants needed to aid recovery, plants not available in most fenced pastures.

Horses that have been kept a long time by Gypsies are often paragons, treated as one of the family. We have known them so powerful and willing that they will pull a waggon over hill and dale with the regularity of a traction engine, yet so gentle that they will lie on the ground while the infants crawl over them. We've seen a Smith *chavvy* (child), stroll fearlessly between the shaggy fore-legs of a grazing horse and put a loving arm around each. When her mother called her away it was with 'Stop botherin' the horses!'

THE WAGGON

Internal facilities usually attract the *gaujo's* first attention, but the externals are more important. For example, the turntable or ring-plates of the fore-carriage or lock should be wide to afford maximum stability when in motion, and the wheels should be large but not heavily built. Pneumatic tyres are of no help. On soft ground their wide base may be useful but on the road it drags, especially with a heavy van. Some travellers fit motor wheels but only because they have found replacements of the traditional kind too hard to come by or too expensive. The fore-carriage is such that by side-stepping the horse till he is under the side window the waggon can be spun around almost in its own length, either forward or in reverse. But on uneven or soft ground this can be dangerous and is the commonest cause of overturning.

Though there are some vans without them, a good brake is almost indispensable. It operates on the two hind wheel-rims from a brass wheel on the footboard. A good horse will hold a van on a hill by sitting back in the shafts, but the brake is still needed to take weight off the breeching strap. On a down gradient it can be adjusted to minimise tension on either the breeching or the traces.

To hold the van down steep hills there is the skid-pan, drag or slipper. This iron 'shoe' is attached by a heavy chain to the swivel-pin of the lock. It hangs on a hook at the back of the fore-carriage and on bad hills is placed under the nearside back wheel. There are other safety measures for supplementing the brake. One is a short length of chain with a snap-hook hitched through the spring-iron in front of the nearside back wheel; in an emergency it can be hooked around the wheel rim to lock the wheel. Or you can pull back on short ropes, or walk behind the back wheel holding a kettle-iron down against the rim by levering against the spring scroll-iron. One Gypsy family we know had a large rubber tyre that came off an old Lancaster bomber; they kept it stowed on the cratch until starting downhill, whereupon they threw it overboard to drag behind on a chain from the back axle! The children rode on it, sitting around the rim to make weight. Yet with all this safety-first ingenuity it is horse management that matters. On a steep hill, without his help, you can drag both hind wheels and yet get out of control.

For travelling uphill a useful attachment is a roller or scotch. Held by light chains from the hub-cap and axle-case, this iron-shod cylindrical chock can be hooked in position to jingle along behind the near back wheel. It takes the weight of the van on a hill if the horse should unexpectedly stop halfway. In lieu of a roller, a block of wood on a stick is often kept on the cratch for the same purpose. It's a good thing to have handy in any event, for if a horse jibs badly on a hill the van can jump the roller and it needs fast work with a block to avoid disaster.

Strap or van harness is always used. The shafts of a *vardo* are not designed for chain harness like farmers used. Strap harness comprises: (a) a bridle fitted with blinkers and a double ring snaffle bit; (b) a collar with thick leather traces attached which run back to the trace hooks at the base of the shafts; (c) the pad with wide tug-loops on the pack strap to hold the shafts up and the girth or belly-band; and (d) the crupper strap for the tail, fastened to the back of the pad, from which the breeching is suspended with tug-straps that buckle around the shafts and traces through the breeching staples. All straps—throat-strap, back-strap, belly-band, etc —have a buckle on both sides so that the harness can be adjusted to fit. Finally a set of full-length, stitched leather reins (fourteen feet long) are passed through the rings on the pad and collar-harness and buckled through the double rings on the snaffle. Long reins are essential for driving from footboard or curb. Gypsies like to use decorated harness with ram's-horn hames, horse-shoe buckles, pendants of red patent leather and silver, brass or white-metal in mountings (see plate page 107). A coach-whip was often carried, banded with brass down the length of the stock.

THE PITCH

Many travellers go into winter quarters in the autumn and are usually provided with accommodation by friends should they have none of their own. Yet some continue to travel in cold weather. Then they must move on to where the grass is not eaten down, for it is cumbersome to carry fodder. When the grass is rank a move is necessary every seven to fourteen days, and a suitable day is chosen to move to *puv* the *grai*, to pasture the horse. The space necessary is a circle about sixty feet in diameter, that is, for thirty feet of plug chain of which one end is staked and the other hooked to a strap about the horse's neck. In winter one circle of this size suffices at most for one day only, after which the pin must be pulled and moved to another position.

The ideal pitch, pull-in or 'atchin'-place'—never 'camp' or 'encampment'—is on reasonably firm and level ground. Mud is the waggon's great enemy. The horse that cannot pull forward pushes back and puts a strain on the shaft framing which is usually the first thing to suffer if the wheels get dug in. Then increased horse-power is the only sure remedy.

To a good pitch a nearby water supply is desirable and often essential, a pond or stream within riding or walking distance. Although water jacks may be filled when passing through a village people not unusually refuse water to Gypsies and, anyway, there is a limit to the amount that jacks can carry.

It will be clear from this that, quite apart from the severe and harassing limitations of the Law, good pitches are infrequent and have been as well known to generations of travellers as are stations to railway passengers. Yet no map has ever been made of them, and their names have an archaic ring: Little Egypt is met with all over Britain, and others that come to mind are Gallows Grove, Dooval's Oak, Rushy Gap, Frogs-and-Toads Forest, Dead Sophie's Lane—these are a fair sample.

THE DAY ON THE ROAD

Travelling in traditional style is more like overlanding than holidaying, however it may look to the *gaujo*. It may be easy, it may be difficult, depending on the road conditions and the behaviour of the horse, that servant of the Gypsy from time immemorial. He may be schipzophrenic even though he may have learned to pull at his mother's side and was a four-year-old before being entrusted with his own waggon. The actual travelling is not itself a way of life, but a means to an end, a means often dangerous. It is not at all unknown, when difficult country is anticipated, for the womenfolk to take the children by safer means—bus or train. Demanded above all is the ability to improvise, often at a moment's notice.

The times of start and arrival are determined by weather, kind of traffic expected and distance of destination. The procedures of start and arrival vary little, bar accidents, but what happens in between depends also on seasons of year, part of country traversed, its people, its industries, and the occupations at the moment of the members of the travelling family. So that, while departure and arrival are capable of a fair summary here, the interim is comprised of too many variables to permit of equivalent description.

The traveller's day on the road starts with one of the older men rising early to re-light the stick fire still burning from the previous night. He rakes the white ash from its sides, exposes the charcoal and gently blows on it. It quickly revives, and he adds *koshties*, little sticks kept dry beneath the waggon. If night rain has dowsed the fire, making a new one is as second nature to the old man; with a little paper, a few *koshties* and perhaps a handful of small coal, he brings the kettle to the boil faster than the housewife on her gas ring.

For people who are used to it, a stick fire is a most efficient way of cooking. In the last century the kettle was suspended from a 'chittie' or tripod, but about 1900 the tripod began to be superseded by the kettle-iron—a bent crowbar of which the pointed, straight base is thrust securely into the ground at such an angle that the top end, hook-fashioned, is immediately above the fire. Very large tripods are still commonly used by Gypsies in Continental countries, where they travel in tribes rather than in groups based on the family, as they have always done in Britain.

The kettle singing, the family rises to a cup of tea—the standard beverage—followed by a substantial if makeshift breakfast, for there is no knowing when or where the next meal will be. The main meal of the day is in the evening, the cooking done then.

In the *vardo* the wife tidies the beds. She makes all fast within. She takes down the lamp from its bracket and stows it in the cupboard. She secures every item liable to break by being thrown to the floor by jolting that sometimes seem to reach earthquake proportions. Crockery, glass, china ornaments, photographs, all the family treasures are put away in drawers between soft fabrics.

Outside, the bender is dismantled and the tent beds are rolled and secure on the cratch, or loaded onto a flat-cart. The sooty utensils are not carried in the van but placed in the pan-box. The bantams are crated up and stowed. With more than one living waggon in the party, a pan-box is perhaps used for the bantams, and on a Ledge or Bow-top van a chicken or two may be placed in the hinged-door spindle racks. Bantams, by the way, are the class of poultry usual in a Gypsy menage. They are small and hardy, and know the ways of the road from chicks. Vans often start to move off and leave them to catch up the hay-filled pan-box, racing after their home in alarm. The cockerels are sturdy fighters, and a good one is highly prized. We knew of one bantam cock that was reputedly raffled fifty times by its owner at pubs along the road. Each time he bought it back from the winner for a fraction of the takings!

Cage birds and cats are not uncommon, but a Gypsy entourage without the protection of a dog or two is exceptional. The favourite is the lurcher, an intelligent cross-breed, usually between greyhound and collie, much used for poaching rabbits and hares. They are excellent waggon guards while the owner is away and, on the road, are quite at home walking on leash behind the waggon at a safe, slow place, though they often ride up inside or on one of the carts.

Horses out of harness like to roll and, if they are muddy, are rubbed down before taking the road. The steps are unhooked from the footboard, and carried back and hung from the hooks below the cratch, or they may be placed on the floor of the van or on a flat-cart. With chain still on, the waggon horse is led up to the shafts from his grazing ground; the harness is taken down from its stowage place, hung clear of the ground on a stick passed through the rear wheels. The horse is then 'dressed up', harnessed, and backed into the shafts, which are threaded through the tug loops on the back-strap. The traces are then unrolled, taken back and hooked into the trace hooks at the shafts' base; and finally the long reins are threaded through rings on the saddle and collar, and buckled to the snaffle rings on the bit.

A glance around to see whether all are near-ready to move, then off with the brake. To start a heavy van rolling on the road, or pulling off the soft ground, a good horse doesn't jerk into the harness. He sways forward on his legs till he feels the traces tighten, then squats with hind legs bent and leans slowly into the collar, using his own weight and muscle with an understanding and deliberation that are good to see. The driver manoeuvres with care off the pitch and onto the macadam, his back to the road, leading the horse and watching wheels and curb to avoid the waggon being thrown about. At a suitable distance he pulls it up to await the others in the party.

By now the fire has died down. Strictly it should be dowsed but often is not, though a Gypsy's fire is rarely anything but safe—his vans and tents are too close and vulnerable for risk. It must be admitted that many travellers leave their piches in bad shape, but the more intelligent make a point of cleaning up well and do so out of enlightened self-interest. Unfortunately the well-tidied pitch is rarely identifiable as such. It is the badly left one that advertises itself.

The pitch clear of all its occupants and their belongings, the Gypsy leaves his *patteran* to indicate that he has been there and whence he has gone. Such signs are legion, known and understood only by travellers themselves; a sod cut at a corner, a hazel stick banded in a certain way to indicate the number of waggons and pointing in a clear direction. To follow a *patteran* is the Romany equivalent of following a blazed trail. By this and other kinds of relay system, primitive but effective, travellers' news flies far and fast.

The timing of the journey matters. If the objective is a one-night pitch, an early arrival risks being moved on. A day's travel may be two or three miles only and, thought sixty per day have been known, twenty approaches the normal maximum. At a convenient time and place it is usual for the womenfolk to leave to 'go calling', to sell their wares from door to door, often walking many miles in a day. This accomplished, and with the proceeds, they go shopping, filling their empty baskets with whatever is needed on a day-to-day basis; there is too little room to keep reserve provisions. Then they re-join the men at some place pre-arranged, often taking bus or train to it. In case of unforeseen difficulty an alternative is agreed on or a *patteran* left at the rendezvous. Generally speaking, Gypsies keep to parts of the country and roads that they are accustomed to, travelling further afield only when some special reason requires it.

Meanwhile, the waggon and its auxiliaries may be rolling at a fast walking pace over the fifteen or twenty miles of the journey. There will be a rest mid-day for two hours or so, and exchanges of news with friends and acquaintances along the road. There are rests at the tops of hills and at pubs and other convenient places, where no opportunity is lost of a *chop*—the Gypsy is a born trader. But, apart from the mid-day siesta and feed, the horses stay in the shafts until the journey's end, when they 'dror in' onto the new pitch and are unhooked. The horses, by the way, are watered along the road, that is, before rather than after feeding.

Down shafts, with each horse staked out on its thirty-foot chain, the *chavvies* go off *kettering koshties* for the *yog*. The birds are let out, the fire is lit, the kettle on, the bender pitched, the family treasures in the *vardo* returned to their shelves, the bracket lamp reinstated. Soon the womenfolk, back from their marketing, are preparing the evening meal. Like breakfast, it is usually cooked on the stick fire, for the stove is used only in winter, in wet or windy weather, or if someone is ill.

In the evening, smartened up, some of the family go out

'driving' in trap or flat-cart to a pub, cinema or other attraction, and the women with them 'dress up'. If the intended stay on the pitch is for a few days or more, pegs are whittled from hazel rods, life-like chrysanthemums are fashioned from elder, baskets woven from willow or strips of split hazel, and other handicrafts are prepared to provide goods to sell during the time there. For baskets there is still a ready sale though making them is a dying craft. For pegs there was a good demand till about 1955 when durable snag-free plastic types became widely available. Today the wooden pegs still have their devotees but they are unobtainable in most districts now, and the Gypsy woman is more likely than not to offer artificial flowers or the products of factories. The travellers' way of life is changing fast—whose is not?

This chapter is not so much intended to describe a typical traveller's life on the road today (though it is still true of some) but rather to indicate something of the daily round and common task of Gypsy waggon-dwellers over the last two generations or so. Without some appreciation of the kind of life that the *vardo* has served and still serves it is impossible to come to any understanding of our subject. Perhaps, preoccupied with fact, we have conveyed too little of its spirit. For this we refer the reader to the bibliography, and especially to *The Gorse and the Briar* by Patrick McEvoy, the down-to-earth books of *vardo*-living Dominic Reeve, and to the autobiography of the leading English Gypsy of our time, Silvester Gordon Boswell.

Page 71 A Dunton-built Reading still in regular use in 1967, Fred Walker up

Page 72 (above) A fine Ledge waggon by Tong Herons at Brough Fair in the 1920s; *(below)* typical Ledge waggon by Wright, *circa* 1910

CHAPTER FOUR

THE BASIC TYPES

In Chapter One we differentiated between a Gypsy caravan as a class of living waggon, and a caravan lived in or owned by Gypsies. Its style remains throughout its life but its ownership or use passes. We defined its broad characteristics and on these we shall now elaborate, but will deal with them more technically in later chapters.

With the exception of the modern Open-lot, only minor variations in design occurred after about 1910. Even home-made vans—'peg-knife waggons', supposedly shaped up with the aid of that tool—tended to emulate the desirable features of those professionally built. However, it was not uncommon for a traveller to add to or to remove features of an old waggon, re-mount a body on underworks other than its own, or replace unsound wheels by ones that differed in weight, size or structure from the original, so altering the proportions of the whole. Few waggons over sixty or so years of age have survived in the form in which they were first built.

There are six design types (of which the five extant ones, plus an ancillary vehicle are illustrated in Fig 1). They are known by various names but are perhaps best called the Reading, the Ledge and the Bow-top—the most typically Romany; the now extinct Brush—characteristic of brush, broom, rush and wickerwork makers; the Burton—most

73

typically showman; and, the only modern one, the Open-lot. There are two ancillaries, not properly living waggons, the four-wheeled and the two-wheeled tilted pot carts. The first attempt to categorise Gypsy vans was made by Mr Ferdinand Huth in the *Journal* of the Gypsy Lore Society thirty years ago, and we found that we can do little better than accept and expand on his definitions, with the addition of the Open-lot.

Being individually built, no two waggons are exactly alike. They vary according to customer requirements, price, skill and location of builder, and period. At the same time they have certain exterior features in common, and with few exceptions the interiors conform to a set plan or layout. Thus, the *vardo* is always one-roomed on four high wheels, with door and movable steps in front (the Brush waggon the only exception), sash windows, a rack called the 'cratch' and a pan-box at the rear.

Inside a waggon the atmosphere is snug and homely, and the finer vans have an almost regal splendour. Almost everything one needs is to hand. Even in winter you need never be cold. The fire in the stove, if built up with windows closed for half an hour, will so heat the rails near the roof that they will be too hot to hold. One of the Coopers once claimed that he could bake a cake in his van by stoking up the fire, shutting the windows, and leaving the mixture in a tin on the table!

Because the cubic space is small, condensation calls for ventilation on the lee side, but this problem is hardly more serious than in a cottage room. Still, it must be confessed that, compared with the house dweller, the inmates of a van do suffer two deficiencies—the privy *is* external, and a bath may be had only by friendly invitation, resort to a public bath house, or by opportunistic improvisation. But there are compensations, and no domicile is perfect.

Inside the waggon the cabinet work may be either dark red

polished mahogany or stained pine, and the walls are grained or scumbled in light golden-brown. In vans that have had a lot of wear and tear the original wood finish has often been painted or grained over.

Internal layout, which varies little from type to type or van to van, has not changed for a century. The basic needs of the residents are the same and, in such confined space, there is only one sensible way to meet them. The entrance is frontal and half-doored. Through it, and on your immediate left, you find a tall, narrow wardrobe and beneath it perhaps a small brush cupboard. The fireplace stands next, and is always on the left as you enter, for on that side the chimney pipe is in less danger from roadside trees. From a point about two feet above the top of the stove (described more fully in Chapter Seven) the fireplace is boxed in to form an airing cupboard. On the front of this cupboard and above the fireplace is a brass-railed shelf and next comes the offside window, and beneath a locker seat for two.

To the right, as you enter, is a bow-fronted corner cupboard; the top part, usually having glass doors, is probably used for displaying china, and the cupboard below for boots and cleaning gear. Opposite the fire there is another locker seat, and of a cold winter's day it is good to sit there, lean back and place your stockinged feet on the brass guard rail on the front of the stove. Next to the seat is a bow-fronted chest of drawers.

Filling the back of the van is a two-berthed bed-place, the top bunk just below the rear window, and beneath it are two sliding doors. These in the daytime shut away a second, shorter bed-place in which the children sleep.

Light is supplied from a bracket oil-lamp above the chest of drawers, the surface of which is used as a table. More light may come from candles. One evening we were discussing lighting with one of the Smiths. We idly observed: 'The good

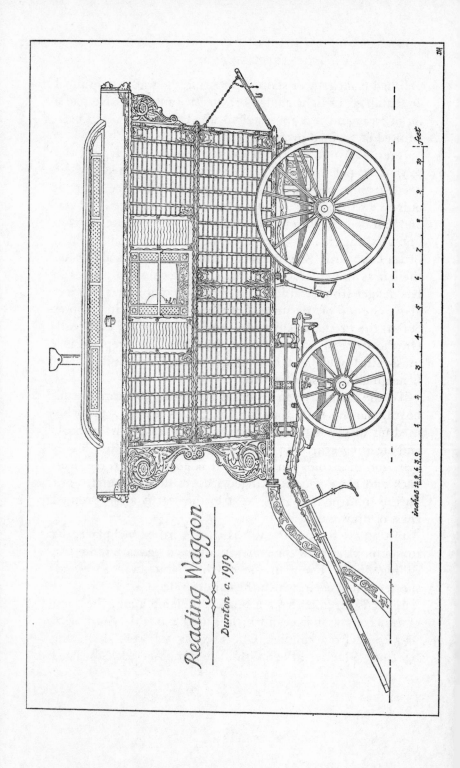

Reading Waggon

Dunton c. 1919

inches 12.9.6.3.0   1   2   3   4   5   6   7   8   9   10   feet

Reading by Dunton

front

rear

(Shafts and cratch omitted for clarity)

thing about these mirrors with the candles in front of them is that you get double the light out of one candle.'

'No,' Smith retorted, 'it don't make no difference, do it?'

'Why not?'

'Well,' he said, 'if you got anuvver candle in the glass you got anuvver waggin too, look, what's for to be lighted up.'

The internal layout which is described above is not the result of imposed standardisation, of course, but was evolved over a period by many different makers, the placing of each item having been found to be best. Most extant waggons conform to it. Similarly, while all waggons are predominantly of one type or another, some originally combined features from two or even more types. Vans were not designed to fit a premeditated category recorded in a pattern book, but were built to suit the needs of the purchaser. Builders came to be known for one or other kind of van but built whatever was required of them.

The Reading, established by the Dunton family at Reading, Berkshire, but made by various builders, is slung between tall wheels and is straight sided with a pronounced outward slope from floor to roof (see plate pages 53, 54 and scale drawings pages 76, 77). The body is of beaded tongue-and-groove match-board with upright chamfered ribs. It has a high-arched roof, since about 1900 built with concealed gutters and a clerestory skylight of the mollicroft kind (Fig 4). Some, made to order for well-to-do customers, are luxurious and lavishly carved and gilded inside and out. Poorer travellers had to be content with carving limited to the front and rear porch-brackets, but the basic design is always the same: sloping walls and wheels outside the body. It is the type most liked by Gypsies and the home most characteristic of a good Romany family.

The earliest pictures show a somewhat austere design (see

plate page 17), sometimes with the rib construction apparently on the inside, a plain arched roof with no skylight, no gutters, and the carving restricted to small triangular brackets supporting the porches fore and aft. Around 1885 vans appeared with corner stanchions that had been lathe-turned, porch-brackets carved in a three-dimensional design of flowers, leaves and entwined stems, and carved pieces between the ribs along the bottom sills and under the eaves. The windows were divided into many panes and the shutters into elaborately moulded panelling.

Although somewhat decorative and graceful, these early versions look rather prim and pokey. Sometimes they were nicknamed 'kite waggons' from the high arched roof and sloping sides.

One of the last Dunton Reading waggons in regular use on the road was lived in by the Romany horse dealer, 'Norfolk' Fred Walker, with his wife and young family (see page 71) till he sold it in 1967 to a dealer and one-time traveller. It was renovated and further embellished at great cost, overturned, restored once more and travelled the road again for a time till sold to an antique dealer for the reputed sum of £4,000. It appears occasionally at carnival or rally.

The Ledge is sometimes called the Cottage waggon (see scale drawings, pages 80 and 81). It has a narrow base with upright sides, but from a point about 18in from the floor the body is built out on ledges over the wheels to a width similar to that of the Reading (see plate page 72). The ledges are reinforced by scrolling brass supports which rest on projecting cross-beams at floor level. The match-boarding of the side walls projects front and back and is cut to form the porch-brackets, which are decorated with pieces of carving, usually gilded, and strengthened by a thin iron brace curved to the shape of the brackets.

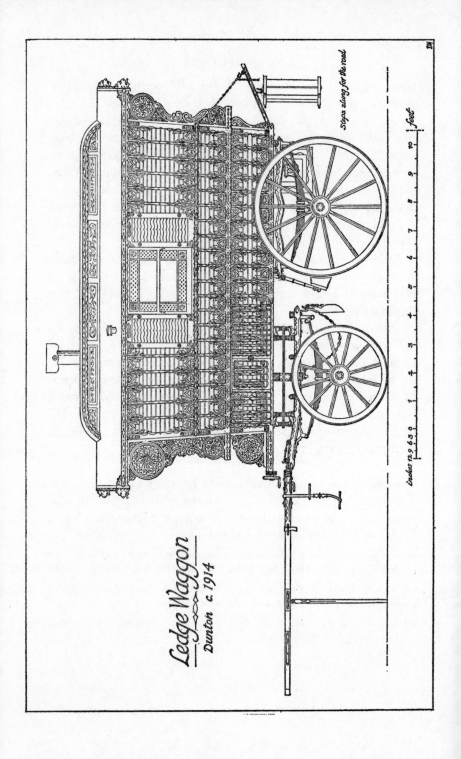

Ledge Waggon

Dunton c. 1914

Steps slung for the road

Inches 12 9 6 3 0   1   2   3   4   5   6   7   8   9   10   feet

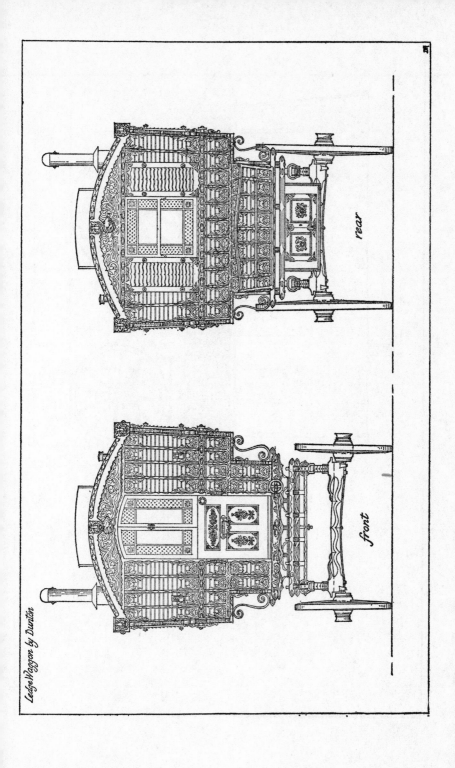

Ledge Waggon by Duntön

rear

front

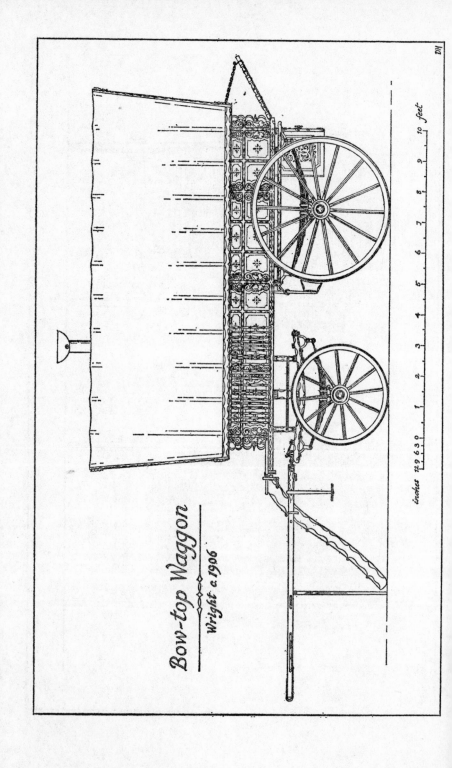

Bow-top Wagon

Wright c.1906

inches 12 9 6 3 0   1   2   3   4   5   6   7   8   9   10 feet

DH

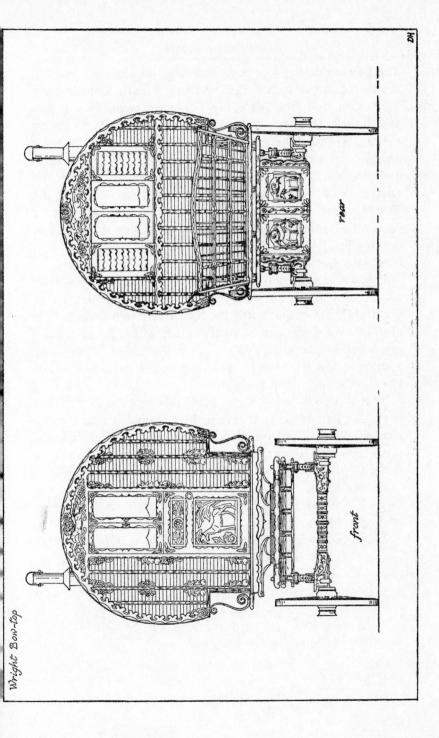

Wright Bow-top

rear

front

DH

The Bow-top design (see scale drawings on pages 82 and 83) is also variously called the Midland, Leeds, Lincolnshire, Yorkshire, Bell and Barrel-top (see plate pages 89 and 90). It is built with ledges like a Ledge waggon, but has a round canvas top on a bowed wood frame. The front and back walls are built rib-and-matchboard style, with carved crown-boards and pieces of carving between the chamfered ribs. Inside, the roof is lined with a patterned chenille stretched over the framing immediately beneath the canvas. This type has a rather dark interior due to the absence of side windows but for comfort, lightness of weight and durability combined it is unequalled by any other.

It was especially popular with Gypsies because it combined elegance with lightness, durability and a low centre of gravity. Of all waggons it is the least likely to overturn. It is also the least conspicuous, an advantage when camping near, say, a well-keepered estate: the green sheet blended with the hedgerow and the absence of side windows rendered it less likely to be noticed at night.

This type was built in the Midlands and the North, but never for showmen. It is erroneously supposed that it originated in Ireland, from the profusion there of 'barrel-tops' lining the roadsides at the summer fairs, 'bodged-up vans for poverty tinkers', as an English Romany once haughtily described them. Irish vans of this kind were inferior to the English, and Irish travellers who could afford to do so came to England to buy their vans.

There is also what may be described as a sub-type of the Bow-top. It is normally referred to as a Square Bow (see plate page 107). As the name implies, its canvas top is on a square instead of a bowed frame, and it was usually Gypsy-built on a tradesman's waggon. Square Bows were occasionally made to order by established builders on a cart brought into the yard by a traveller for the purpose.

The Brush, sometimes called a Fen waggon, was the home of the original door-to-door brush salesman. It is a descendant of the kind possibly used by Old Fulcher, in Borrow's *The Romany Rye*, circa 1825, and is believed to be extinct (see plate pages 108 and 125). It is straight-sided, with wheels outside the body like the Reading, but has no skylight. Its internal fittings are not dissimilar from those of other types. It has two distinctive characteristics: the half-door and glazed shutters are at the back instead of the front as in all other Gypsy vans, together with steps that are a fixture; and the exterior is equipped with spindled racks and glazed cases to accommodate brushes and brooms of various kinds and sizes, rush mats, baskets and other wickerwork articles made from sedges, willow, birch and similar materials indigenous to heath or marshland. Running all around the roof are three light iron rails, and sometimes trade-name boards, used for stowing bulkier goods.

This type was used mainly by *poshrats* and *didikais* who made and traded in such wares, chair-mending, etc. In the 1920s it was succeeded by the motor brush-waggon. Before the spread of the penny bazaar, these travellers were one of the main sources from which housewives bought their brushes, mats and baskets, and many cottages and farmhouses had their rush-bottomed chairs and wicker furniture.

The Burton design (see plate pages 125 and 126, and scale drawings pages 86, 87) is often called the Showman, but Burton is preferable as it differentiates it from the heavy coach-like showmen's waggons pulled by several horses or an engine—'Showman Specials', not classifiable as Gypsy caravans.

Orton and Spooner at Burton-upon-Trent, Staffordshire, were especially noted for it, and excellent ones were built by Howcroft of Hartlepool, Durham, Watts of Bridgwater, Somerset, and others. It is straight-sided but with wheels

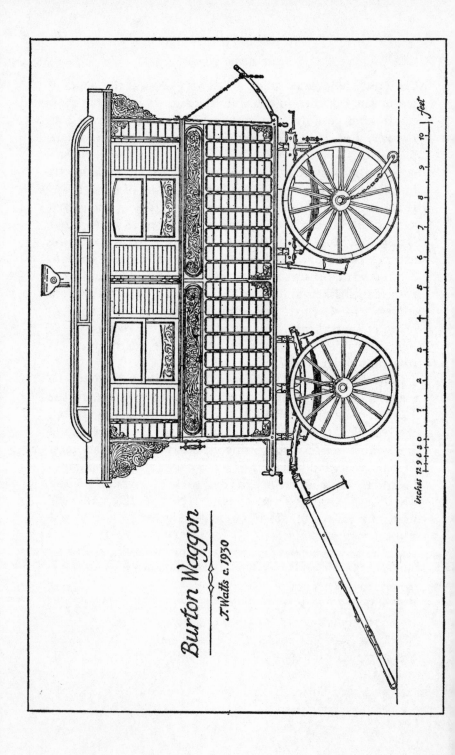

Burton Waggon

J. Watts c. 1930

inches 12 9 6 3 0   1   2   3   4   5   6   7   8   9   10 | feet

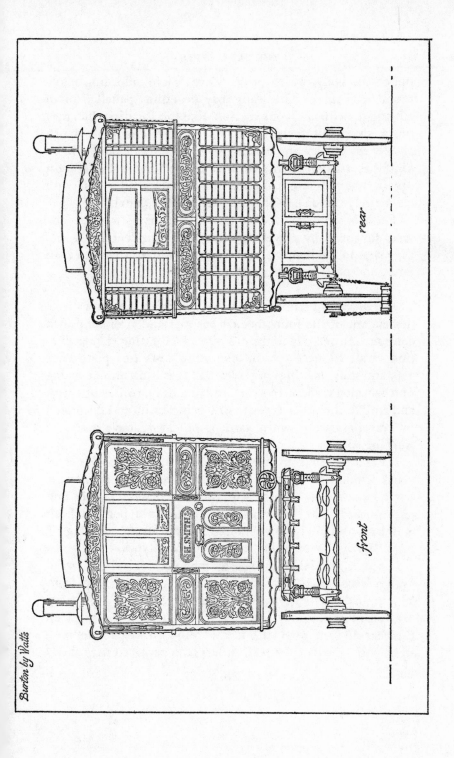

Burton by Watts

front

rear

under the body, which projects over them, affording maximum floor space. The walls may be either panelled or of rib-and-matchboard construction, like the Reading, but they never slope out more than two inches. The roof, which always has gutters and a skylight, sometimes of the Pullman kind, has a flatter arch than that of the Reading. The most ornate waggons are panelled front, back and sides, with elaborately carved oak plaques fixed to each panel.

Though sometimes Gypsy-owned, this type was the one most favoured by travelling showmen; unlike the Gypsies they kept to the high-roads, did not need high wheels to cross fords, and preferred the greater floor space.

The Open-lot, sometimes called the Yorkshire Bow, is a direct descendant of the four-wheeled pot cart and is of simplified construction relative to the old types, facilitating standardisation rendered necessary by mounting costs (see plate page 143, and scale drawings pages 92, 93). It is built on an existing four-wheeled tradesman's cart, called a dray, trolley or lurry; and unlike the other types is still being built and decorated by travellers who own a yard or otherwise have access to working space.

It has a bowed, canvas-covered top, a fixed back with shuttered window, a pan-box and cratch, and an open frame front, whence its name, with decorated side panels and crown-board. The bow roof projects to form porches front and back but there is no footboard. Its layout (see Fig 19, page 166) differs somewhat from the earlier types.

It was established as a type by the 1930s, when the last of Wright's pot carts were showing signs of wear. The front at first had a single, upright, chamfered pillar supporting the centre of the bow, and the front board was dipped on the near side and shod with metal nosing to facilitate stepping in from the steps or shafts. Builders later replaced the central

Page 89 (above) Open-lot and Flat-cart with an accommodation top; *(below)* a renovated Bow-top by Hill

Page 90 (above) Bow-top by Wright, early 1900s, with sunflower decoration on door; *(below)* a later style of Wright-built Bow-top, *circa* 1910

pillar with two pillars about 2ft 2in apart, which ran up to a decorated crown-board, and the dip in the front board was placed in the centre. At about the same stage the bow was extended forward to form a porch complete with chamfered weatherboard and lined with match-boarding as on the Bow-top. A porch was also extended at the rear and the detachable matchboard back became a fixture, with all the decorative features and 'couterments', shutters, etc, of a Bow-top. Fixed furniture was now installed inside, along with the stove and the characteristic, vertical, glass-fronted cupboards on either side of the bow at the front of the van. These rested on the ledges and were tall enough to contain three square shelves for crockery. The last stage of the evolution was the fitting of decorated panels at the sides of the bow in front, to shield the front cupboards, and the Open-lot became almost as proud, self-contained and decorative as a regular Bow-top van.

Demand for this type of van still continues from travelling people who are confirmed traditionalists and from those who retain horses. It is often used by dealers as a summer waggon for visiting such horse fairs as Appleby, and by others for fruit and other seasonal cropping.

The open front makes for pleasant travelling, as everyone riding up is able to view the unfolding landscape. An Open-lot can be snug enough even in winter. In inclement weather specially fitted canvas curtains, hooked around the bow beneath the front porch, can be hooked back or reefed shut with a tie rope. For added privacy and warmth a curtain is sometimes hung inside the open front.

Although they are not living waggons in the sense in which we use the term, not being equipped as homes and therefore not Gypsy caravan types, there are two ancillary vehicles, sleeping carts, that have commonly been used for many years, longer than living waggons proper, and it is appropriate to

F

Open-lot
I. Barras c. 1965

inches 12 9 6 3 0   1   2   3   4   5   6   7   8   9   10 feet

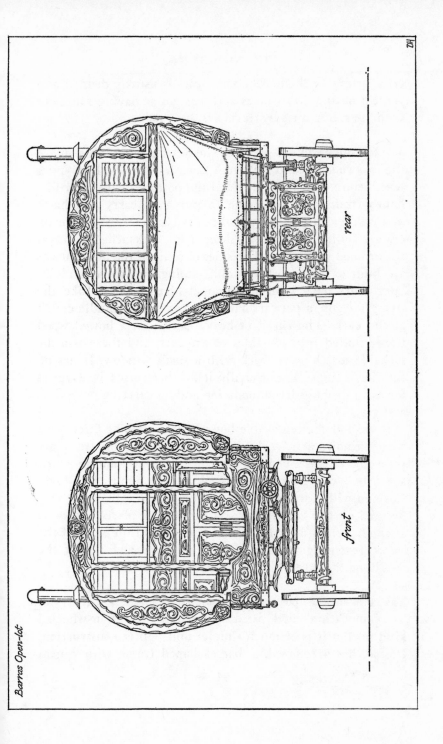

Barrus Open-lot

rear

front

refer briefly to them. The word *cart* is usually defined as a vehicle having two wheels and *waggon* as having four, but both are called carts by travellers.

The four-wheeled tilted pot cart: the older name of this and of the two-wheeled kind is Potter's Cart, from its use by Gypsies who, before the canals provided the potteries with their first hauled transportation, came to purchase, carry and hawk around the country cheap and faulty earthenware. It is elaborately built, boat-shaped, fitted with a detachable canvas tilt or hood (see Fig 1). The sides of some of the older makes are built of open-work spindle framing, but those made in later years have solid rib-and-matchboard sides. Like the living waggon, a pot cart has a pan-box and a spindle cratch at the back. The tilt is of heavy canvas on a bowed wood frame slotted into the sides of the cart, and there is a detachable match-board back with a small window. It has no interior fittings. Traditionally it has been used by Gypsies for extra sleeping accommodation and for carrying provisions and gear.

Instead of the removable bowed tilt, it may be fitted with what is known as a 'Yorkshire accommodation top' (see plate page 89). This is a bed box 6ft x 3ft 10in x 9in high, to which are fitted four hoops from head to foot about $4\frac{1}{2}$ft high. Covered with a waggon sheet and holding a palliasse, it may be used on the ground but, on the cart, is placed crosswise at the front, its short legs falling just within the sides of the cart, preventing it from sliding sideways and taking the weight off the rave which it overhangs either side.

The two-wheeled pot cart is sometimes loosely called an 'accommodation' and is distinct from the four-wheeled kind in that it is of much simpler and lighter construction. It, too, has a removable, barrel-shaped frame with canvas

94

tilt and an accommodation top or let-down bed. The back, also, is of match-board with window, and the front has canvas curtains. There are many variants of it, more or less shaped up according to need and taste. It is probably the oldest kind of wheeled conveyance used by travellers. Usually it has struts to the shafts and others at the rear so that, unhorsed, it may stand in a level position, usually more securely maintained by poking the shafts into a hedge.

CHAPTER FIVE

NOTABLE BUILDERS

Building Gypsy caravans may at one time have promised to be a worth-while business, but it called for more than craft skills, not least an ability to deal with the travelling people and their ways. Not all wheelwrights with the requisite know-how would have had the patience, shrewdness and strength of character, indeed physique, to stand up to the here-to-day-gone-tomorrow roughnecks of the road and many must have shared the common prejudice against Gypsies or found themselves unable to provide the unusual services that they expected. Those who did establish reputations worked in localities frequented by travellers—in towns and villages with or near horse fairs or fruit, vegetable and hop picking; or by showmen in centres convenient for lucrative tours.

To be remembered, a productive enterprise needs to have had a substantial output over a long period and preferably some lasting record of its activities made during or soon after its lifetime. However, scarcely any records of caravan builders exist, and only a few builders are remembered today. Even by 1914 the numbers of craftsmen engaged were shrinking, and by now almost all the few even young men then working have died or been forgotten. With few exceptions they were not people to have been noticed in print, even to have received the modest distinction of an obituary in a local newspaper. Accordingly, we have traced few survivors whose skills are family-inherited from the Edwardian hey-day of the caravan and whose memories are reliable.

Nevertheless, it is possible to put together a picture of the kinds of craftsmen engaged, how they went about their work, their difficulties and how they overcame or were overcome by them. The facts about these few at least throw some light into the corners of this obscure Victorian industry.

THE SOUTHERN AND EASTERN COUNTIES

The name most often recalled is *Dunton and Sons*, of Reading, Berkshire, whose productions survive in some numbers. It is not known whether they were the originators of the Reading type although they almost certainly established it. One of the best publicly owned examples is in the Bristol City Museum; another, a Ledge, is in the possession of the Reading Borough Museum; a third, *circa* 1905, and once in the Buckland family, that was closely connected with Hampstead Heath Fair, is preserved at Kenwood House by the Parks Department of the Greater London Council.

Dunton's superlative Reading, Burton and Ledge waggons were fairly diverse in design but their underworks remained constant over many years, from as early as 1880, and are distinguishable by their slender, arched axle-cases cut with generous 18in butterfly chamfers and surmounted by bridged spring-blocks. The Dunton family built primarily for *Romani foki*, Irish travellers and English (non-Romany) travellers; considerably less for showmen.

The firm occupied premises in Reading from at least 1874 when 'Dunton and Son' is listed in local directories as 'coach and cart wheelwright and general smith' at 30 King's Road and Highbridge Wharf. It is not known when they made their first caravan but by 1884 they were described as 'van

97

builders'. From 1888 they are recorded plurally as 'Dunton & Sons' and by 1889, as 'coach and carriage builders', they had moved to Crane Wharf, King's Road, where they remained, trading as 'coach and cart wheelwrights, spring and tyre smiths', until the business was sold in 1922 to Froud, Rivers and Kernutt, who later occupied the premises.

The business appears to have been founded by Samuel Dunton, of 30 King's Road, which was adjacent to his business premises at the wharves of the River Kennet. All that we have been able to dicover of him is that 'at 97 he collapsed putting a cart wheel on a wheel horse, and died three days later.' He had three sons: Alfred (1837-1924), after his father the mainstay of the business; Samuel Eber (1848-1823), described in his death certificate as 'formerly a wheelwright'; and William. Various others of the family were engaged in the firm, including Albert (1872-1963), Alfred's son.

Mr Ferdinand Huth remembers from the 1914 period Sam (II) as attending to the business side and making the contracts, and Bill as working in an upstairs shop on the bodies, seated in a chair and doubled up with infirmity, cutting chamfers on pieces of waggon held firm by a wooden clamp between his knees. A nephew, George (d.1921) did the painting and gilding.

Mrs Albert Dunton, Alfred's daughter-in-law, recalls that show people stopped on the Triangle, the fair-ground opposite Reading railway station, while Gypsies stayed on Ascot Heath. They would come in for repairs or to order a new waggon. Sam bought standing timber—oak, ash, elm and walnut; only the pine was imported. The timber was felled and dressed, and brought in horse-drawn drugs to Crane Wharf where it was sawn to requisite size and stacked for five years to season.

No drawings were made. Each job was discussed with the client and specific measurements were noted down on whatever was to hand, often on the back of an opened-out cigarette packet.

The firm employed three smiths, a section of the business that had special attention. They made their own springs, and forge-welded the step-irons, etc; but latterly many of the iron fittings were ready-mades bought through Will Haines, a hardware specialist in the town. Also in later years the wheels were made by a wright at Woodford, Berkshire. All paint was ground and mixed on the premises in a mill. Carving, upholstery and sun-sheets were subcontracted.

Alfred Dunton, who carried on the business after his father, was a dedicated craftsman who made inlaid furniture for his home and even decorated with marquetry the lid of his toolbox. He was the mainspring of the living waggon business. The Gypsies liked him and would sometimes bring him a present of pheasant or hare. When his son Albert won a scholarship he was not permitted to take it up but was ordered by his father into the business, much against his will. Nevertheless, he became a good craftsman and learnt all the skills—joinery, wheelwrighting, smithing, painting and sign-writing. Albert, like his father, got on well with the Gypsies. 'Treat a Gypsy with respect,' he would say, 'and there's no better person.'

In World War I Dunton built and repaired army vehicles and, hostilities over, the Government offered to finance expansion if Alfred would build army motor bodies. He refused. There was no future in mechanised road transport, he said—'I'm sticking to horse-drawn vehicles'. For Albert this was the last straw; he departed, dry-eyed, and went into shopfitting. Years later, in World War II, he used up the tissues between the old sheets of gold leaf for rolling his cigarettes, letting the gold leaf waft away on the wind.

In their last six years Dunton's built six or seven waggons, taking six months to a year to complete. The Gypsies paid in gold sovereigns, five at a time, as the work progressed.

Mr Eric Goodey, of Reading, whose collection of antique vehicles is hired out for film and other purposes, was a contemporary of the Duntons and knew them well. He said: 'To the Gypsies, who played it by ear, it was never "Dunton" but always "Mr Dunkins." ' The Calladines often stopped by. They were 'dressed very flash with black bowler hats, blue suits, great brown boots, and gold pieces on their watch chains.' One Calladine at this time had a superb waggon built for him with wide spokes carved in the form of horses' hind legs, hoofs to the 'fellies', painted grey, black, piebald, spotted and strawberry roan. These, when the wheels rolled, appeared to be pacing hurriedly along the road behind the shaft horses! This van had a double set of spring shafts and was pulled by two hefty greys. It took all day to mount it on its wheels, after a hatful of gold had changed hands.

Their longevity, reputation and high standards never enriched the family and, although they were highly respected, travellers sometimes played tricks on them. For example (we were told) one would put money down on a waggon, and repeatedly call at the yard to keep it coming on. Yet when finished it was allowed to stand idly around, occupying space, unclaimed. In time a relative of the trickster would call in 'by chance'. He then offered and paid less than its worth to 'take it off your hands.' Thus, the original client got his waggon 'on the cheap' and at Dunton's expense.

Dunton's did not confine themselves to living waggons, of course, and before 1914 many horse dealers and hawkers used a high spring cart that they made at about £25. They turned out baker's and dairymen's vans, sweep's carts, vehicles for Huntley and Palmer, the Reading biscuit makers, and a few traps but 'not much stuff for the gentry'. Alfred built one of the town's first horse buses. But it was for their living waggons that they were noted, and their trade in them

F. J. THOMAS,
Coach and Wheel Works,

NEAR THE RAILWAY STATION,

15 to 19, GUILDFORD STREET, CHERTSEY.

Builder of **Living Vans, Round-abouts, Swing Boats,**
Dart and Ring Boards,

UNDERWORKS, STRIKERS, Etc.

ALL KINDS OF APPLIANCES FOR TRAVELLERS & SHOWMEN,
ESTIMATES FREE. —

HOOP-LA MAKER AND PATENTEE,
By Royal Letters Patent 21525, (1908).

Vans, Carts, Trollies, Etc., for all trades and purposes. [P.T.O.

Fig 6 *Builder's trade-card*

extended over the greater part of the country. Froud, Rivers
and Kernutt, their successors, and body builders themselves,
put together a few vans that had been left unfinished when
they took over in 1922, and for some years they repaired
vans but made none of their own.

Among other makers in southern England was *Williams*
of Leighton Buzzard, Bedfordshire, who built Reading and
perhaps other types; and *F. J. Thomas* at Chertsey, Surrey
(see Fig 6) who built especially for showmen. Henry Thomas
was a wheelwright at Chertsey in the 1870s, and from the
1890s Frederick J. Thomas became widely known for his
sturdy underworks, excellent for the larger waggon, well
proportioned for one 10ft 6in long though somewhat heavy
looking for a ten footer. His vans were well-designed, plain
and solid looking, clean and chamfered but otherwise un-
decorated.

In London itself *D. Macintosh* was building in the 1920s

101

at Upper Norwood, a locality which until the expansion of the metropolis early in the nineteenth century had been one of the principal Gypsy resorts in the southern counties, 'on account of its remote and rural character, though lying so handy for both London and Croydon'. It yet has its Gypsy Hill and 'Queen of the Gypsies' pub.

At Guildford, Surrey, before 1914 *William Wheeler* made good waggons. In 1900 he was listed in the town's directory as a coach builder in Commercial and Woodbridge Roads but ceased so to be during World War I. By 1924 'W. J. Wheeler' was a motor engineer in Woodbridge Road. Also south of London was *George Chiles*, of Burgess Hill, Sussex; his name may be found on the hub caps of old vans, and no doubt he was one of several makers in the Sussex Weald and Downland.

In the eastern counties Cambridgeshire had *C. H. King* at Wisbech as well as *Leonard* of Soham who was in business until recently, well-known for good Burtons, his waggons often built on 'Chertsey' unders. In Huntingdonshire was *Fuller* of Saint Ives, a few of whose productions survive from the late nineteenth century, well built and with much good carving. In Norfolk was *Sykes* of Outwell, who made Brush waggons; and at Norwich *Godbolt* whose vans have the motif of 'St George killing the dragon' carved over the door and rear window. Then at King's Lynn was *Frederick Savage,* the master roundabout builder.

Savage set up his own smithy and foundry in 1850 and within twenty years was making the fair-ground equipment for which he became perhaps the most noted source in the country. In 1873 the business became Frederick Savage and Co Ltd, later Savage Brothers Ltd, and in 1911 Savages Ltd. In 1889-90 he was mayor of the town, where there is a public monument to him. He died in 1898. While Savage's must have had an important influence on the building of living

102

waggons and, indeed, made many themselves, these were not so much the traditional Gypsy caravan kind as the heavy Pullman-coach variety. The firm's 1902 catalogue illustrates one of their long showman's vans, pulled by a single horse— a 'horse killer'.

THE WEST COUNTRY

In apple-growing Somerset *Watts* of Bridgwater is remember-ed, especially for good Burtons, panelled and part-panelled, until World War II. Walter Watts was working as a wheel-wright in Prickett's Lane, North Street, by 1883; and by 1897 he had been joined by John Watts, trading in Market Street, where the 1938 directory records W. Watts and Son.

To the north, in Herefordshire, with its fruit orchards and hop gardens, there were various builders, the best remem-bered of whom are *H. Jones and Son* and *George Cox*, both of Hereford. Their work was in the best tradition. Jones, wheelwright and waggon builder, began about 1870 building farm waggons and carts, living waggons and spring carts for Gypsies, hawkers and tradesmen. He built Ledge and Burton types, and on his premises in Blue School Street probably made more horse waggons for showmen than anyone in the south-west. He was over 70 years old in 1910, and the business closed down in 1924. However, at that time George Cox, who had been a Jones apprentice before the war, continued the Hereford tradition by starting up on his own account in Widemarsh Street, building similarly, so that, although there was no firm of Jones and Cox, G. Cox styled himself as 'Late of Jones & Son', and remained in business until the 1960s. He made his last all-timber living waggon, a Burton, for one of the Smiths in 1938 and after 1945 some good square Bow-tops on trollies brought to him by other Gypsy customers. Latterly he restored vans to a high standard including one, a

103

Cox Ledge type, in 1965. Today, retired, with miniature tools fashioned by himself for the purpose, he makes models including the iron-work and perfect wheels.

Mr Cox estimates that altogether he built or renovated some fifty waggons, and built more farm vehicles than he can count. Also he built some modern 'Showman specials', as well as the body of one of the first Rolls-Royce shooting brakes. At one time he had nine employees, and his painter, Mr A. E. Wood, stayed with him for over thirty years. His carver, Mr Gertnor, a local man of German origin, also carved furniture and church timber; his vines and birds on the vans have a distinctly Teutonic quality. At one time Mr Cox had his own blacksmith but later did the work himself.

The largest firm in the West of England that built horse-drawn caravans, though it catered for other than Gypsies, was in Bristol. It was founded in the 1850s by two members of the Quaker family of Fry, and subsequently became the *Bristol Waggon and Carriage Works Co Ltd*. It grew in the second half of the century from repairing farm vehicles to making almost everything on wheels, from barrows and dog carts to steam-rollers and Pullman cars, employing up to a thousand people.

Albert and Theodore Fry first appear in 1857 as implement makers and wheelwrights; ten years later the business became the Bristol Waggon Works, iron-founders and railway wagon builders. They built living vans for showmen, evangelists, building-site workmen, and pleasure caravanners, including Gypsy caravans and the big, sumptuous vans for circus, menagerie and fair-ground owners. It was this firm that Dr Gordon Stables commissioned to build his 'Wanderer', the first pleasure caravan (Chapter Three). They were also the principal builders of vans for colporteurs—the travelling distributors of Bibles and other religious books; they had a preacher's pulpit at the front and the body lettered with texts.

Although well-known for them, their living vans were only
a small part of the firm's output, which embraced dust carts,
Black Marias, vans for Fry's chocolate factory, ambulances,
horse boxes, gun limbers and lifeboat carriages. In the early
1900s they went into the motor-car trade, and closed down in
the mid-1920s. The Bristol Waggon Company was too large
and diversified to typify builders of Gypsy caravans, but the
high standards it applied in the development of horse-drawn
living waggons generally warrant record here.

THE MIDLANDS

The country around Burton-upon-Trent, Staffordshire, has a
long association with travelling showmen, perhaps because it
is so central. E. H. Bostock, that doyen of menagerie proprietors, tells in his autobiography how 'my mother's new
entrance was built at Burton-on-Trent in 1883' and how he
made his debut as proprietor of the Grand Star Menagerie 'at
Tutbury, five miles from Burton-on-Trent where all my waggons had been made'. He calls his own his 'living carriage',
perhaps to distinguish it from the animal waggons.

George Orton, Sons and Spooner, of Burton-upon-Trent,
became prominent suppliers of machinery and equipment
for showmen. They were founded at the beginning of the
present century by George Orton, a wood carver with works
in Meadow Road, and J. Spooner, a coach builder and carver
in Princess Street. Both had worked for Savage's of King's
Lynn, and over the years made scenic railways, bioscope
shows, roundabouts, tropical scenics, novelty rides, etc. They
established their own engineering workshops and today are
light engineers.

In the first thirty years of the century they became widely
known for their superb carving and immaculate living waggons, which included Reading and Ledge types for Gypsies

105

as well as Burtons for showmen. Their quality was rarely excelled. In addition to these traditional kinds they (like Savage's constructed a number of long, outsize, luxury vans for showmen. Their reputation among travellers, however, rests on the Burton, established as a type by George Orton and J. Spooner, and possibly originated by them.

Belper, in Derbyshire, in its day was resorted to for repairs, carving and gilding, and its waggon building flourished for over 150 years. *W. Watson* was building there a century ago, and turned out both Readings and Burtons. One, *Herbert Varney*, served his time with Watson and in 1906 started his own business in Derwent Street, later moving next door to the paintworks of A. Barnes and Son in the main road.

Bill Watson (unrelated to W. Watson) was foreman at Varney's until they closed in 1939, and we are indebted to him for our facts about them. Varney built and repaired the vans, Barnes painted them. Paintwork represented as much as half the cost. Our informant started with Varney in 1926 at 14 years of age, six shillings a week, a shilling a year rise. The customers were mostly Romanies and other travellers (Dedmans, Gaskins, Smiths, Lees and Gormans among them), for whom each year they turned out two or three vans. These included Bow-tops, Burtons and others of rib-and-matchboard construction with wheels under the straight-sided body. They did other work, building dragons, gallopers and cake-walks for fair-grounds, and motor bodies and coffins (the latter especially from October onwards—'most people seemed to die in winter'). The underworks were made by a local wheelwright, Wilfred Bryan, and carving was done by Sid Burbeck of Belper and journeymen. According to Mr Watson, the carving was in yellow pine of pattern-making quality, and brackets with a standard grape motif were priced at £5 per pair.

No plans were used. Templates were made for matching

Page 107 A 'Square Bow' with a 'coloured' horse dressed in typical Gypsy harness

Page 108 Rear of a Brush waggon—from a drawing by R. W. Macbeth ARA

curves, etc, but were not kept and used again. The shape of the curve had to suit the timber available to minimise scrap. All body timber from floor joists to top rails had to be 'free from knots, sap, shakes and waney edges'. Penny-boarding was rebated (lapped), not tongued and grooved, and fixed to the ribs with 1-inch cut nails. Bows were lined under the canvas with black and red drugget—red felt with a black scroll stencil. Window glass was brilliant-cut, having cut designs with the arrises smoothed for polishing.

Barnes worked independently as well as in collaboration with Varney's, and were a three-generation family business. Their clients were mostly travellers, too. Gold leaf was always used—'for the Gypsies it had to be gold'—and Barnes himself did the gilding and lining-out.

Varney's staff was seven at most when work was pressing, including perhaps three journeymen and two apprentices. Including paintwork, a waggon took six months to complete. Gypsies paid cash and were given £1 back 'for the road'. 'Profit?' their one-time foreman said, 'it was more like exchanging money.'

THE NORTHERN COUNTIES

If a North Country Gypsy wanted a van he most likely went to Wright or Hill in Yorkshire, but when a North Country showman needed a one-horse van he would probably go to *Howcroft* of West Hartlepool, Co Durham, whose reputation was second only to Dunton of Reading for quality of construction and design. When required to, the firm made waggons for Gypsies and showmen as well built and carved as any. One excellent survivor is in the Worcester County Museum.

Hallard Howcroft started the business in 1864, and it grew with the community of travellers that thronged the district

around, where there was no shortage of good craftsmen
among the timber port's iron-foundries, smiths, wood-workers
and painters employed largely in ship-building. The North-
east was noted horse country. Every other village and
township held its races; thoroughbred breeding was a local
occupation—Voltigeur, one of the most famous horses of the
century, was raised at Hart. The fairs of the region attracted
travellers from afar, and the seamen, shipwrights and colliers
of Teeside and Wearside had no inhibitions about enjoying
themselves on high days and holidays. The travelling showmen used Hartlepool as their base and as a permanent
address. Billy Purvis (1783-1853), 'Clown and Jester of the
North', lived and died in the town, and many showmen after
him made it their home. The Market Yard was leased out
and used as winter quarters where equipment was repaired
and renovated before taking the road again at Easter. Many
tracts of ground accommodated side-shows and booths, and
menageries and circuses were visitors every summer.

Hallard Howcroft's connection grew. In the 1880s his
premises were at 38 Ouston Street but by 1900 they had
grown to substantial size at the corners of Burn Road, Oxford
Road and Stockton Road, later concentrating at the junction
of Oxford and Stockton Roads on a site now occupied by a car
showroom and garage. There as coach builders, cartwrights,
painters, and blacksmiths the firm built and maintained
waggons and fair-ground equipment as the Howcroft Carriage
and Engineering Company, its principal overlooking the
yard from his house next door. By 1913 Ralph Barber had
succeeded Howcroft in the business which was turned to
light engineering with the decline of horse-drawn vehicles.
It survived World War II into the 1950s.

On the other side of the Pennines in the heart of Lancashire the *Tong* family of Kearsley, near Bolton, enjoyed a
reputation second to none. Sylvester Gordon Boswell, in his

autobiography, recalls that his father, Trafalgar Boswell, owned the second waggon to be built by Tom Tong in the 1890's. It was considered a palace on wheels, he says, 'with the wheels outside'. Tong's last van was made for Emperor Boss in the 1920s, when the business moved into the motor trade, so that they built living vans for thirty or forty years (see plate page 72). Evolving with the times over a century or more from carts to cars, the firm all told has spanned five generations of Tongs—Thomas the First ('Old Tom'), his son Joe, grandson Tom the Second, great-grandson Tom the Third, and great-great-grandson Andrew.

There were family connections with the trade back to 1825, but Old Tom, wheelwright, cart and waggon builder, started on his own account in 1850. He fetched his timber in bulk from the Manchester docks, each consignment taking fourteen days—the journey there and back, plus waiting, selecting and bargaining. He converted and seasoned all timber on the premises at Kearsley, using the kind of sawpit and long cross-cut, with one sawyer up top and the other in the pit, described by George Sturt in his *Wheelwright's Shop*. Like some other builders who were painters, Tom Tong II did all the finest painting himself. He is still remembered working late, candle in one hand and liner in the other, six hours at a stretch, painting scrolls or fine-lining a van's ceiling. Little else about his waggons is remembered by the family today, but it is clear from surviving examples that the Tongs ranked among the best builders of the 1890-1920 period, making Ledge, Bow-top and Reading vans, as well as Burtons, to their own design characteristic and of the highest quality.

However, two Yorkshire builders are not only remembered and respected but can be described in some detail. One was *William Wright* of Spibey Lane, Rothwell Haigh, near Leeds, who established the Bow-top as a distinct type. In the archives of the Castle Museum, York, is the firm's account book for

111

1909-11 provided by his grand-daughter, Mrs E. Miller, to whom we are grateful for information. Also in the museum is a fair example of his work, a Ledge waggon (Fig 7).

William Wright was born in 1844 in Spibey Lane, where the family had lived for a hundred years, his father a gardener and his mother a weaver, strict chapel-goers. He was apprenticed as a joiner. When he was twenty-one a living waggon broke down at the bottom of the lane, and he repaired it. He decided to build vans himself, and started in 1865. Three years later he married; his wife was 'good with money, a saver, and ran a small market garden selling flowers and plants'.

The family house overlooked the premises—a yard, with timber-built joinery workshop, brick wheelwright shop beside it, forge and paintshop. There was also a pond from which water was taken in buckets for shrinking the tyres onto the wheels, and a sawpit where the timber was cut into scants and stacked with spacers for seasoning.

Bill Wright built carts and waggons for market gardeners and other trades but became known for his living waggons. These were mainly of three kinds—Bow-top, Ledge and Reading, and of these the Bow-tops were renowned for their functional elegance (see plate pages 72 and 90). His trade was with well-to-do Romanies, not showmen, and there was always a lot of coming and going in the yard. He succeeded not only by the quality of his work, but because he 'knew how to do things'. Business was done over a table with a glass or two of whisky, and Gypsies were able to stay at Spibey Lane while they waited for repairs and completions. The Gallaghers, for instance, were accommodated at the far end of the paintshop, had carpets down and would invite the Wrights to tea at a table laid with lace cloth, porcelain and silver.

After his waggon was finished one Gypsy, Eza Heron,

stayed on alongside the yard rent-free for two years. He was wealthy, apparently through dealing in carpets, kept rolls of Treasury notes under his pillow and, in an ornament on the mantlepiece, an uncut diamond 'as big as a thrush's egg'. Like most high-born Gypsies, he was fastidious to a fault about washing and the preparation of food. Mrs Miller remembers afternoon tea with him in his waggon when she was a girl, when sandwiches were served with a gilt fork, and in an elegant cup he'd lace his tea with rum. He was always generous to her because (she thought) no money was asked of him for ground rent.

Every deal meant haggling, and the Gypsies invariably expected the Wrights to buy something from them when they paid a bill—'I buy off you, you buy off me'. Bill Wright established his own methods of foiling cheats: work was never started unless a substantial deposit had been put down, and no waggon had the wheels fitted until the final payment had been made. He went to some trouble to please. When a van was required for shipment abroad, to help the customer evade the import duty payable on a new vehicle, he simulated age and use by dusting the brand new paint with wood ash!

Wright prospered and engaged in various projects. At one time he had a quarry, at another he patented a ventilated lavatory pan. Financially the pan failed, as did eighteen houses that he built. Though he himself did all the joinery work on them, he couldn't meet the bills for the materials and in 1903 had to go bankrupt—'done down because he was not an educated man'. Educated or not, he boarded up his most valued possessions at the top of the house, and soon raised his head again, paying his creditors in full. When he died in 1909 his family inherited seven houses, as well as the business.

All his life Bill had kept his two sons Herbert (1879-1952) and Albert (1881-1933) working from six in the morning till eight at night, and when he died they carried on the business, Herbert a first-rate joiner, Albert a blacksmith and painter. Travellers would come with and for their vans from as far afield as Wales, Scotland and southern England. Albert bought the field across the road from the yard for them to pitch on, and took photographs of them as well as pictures of his productions which he sent to enquirers with estimates. He did the painting and lining-out himself, using very free design with styles growing from accidentals. He would joke about inventing a new style when a brush went wrong.

All carving was 'bought' in Leeds—the motifs typical of Yorkshire *vardoes*, the running horse on the crown-board, the standing horse and acanthus on the entrance and pan-box doors, grapes and pears for corners, porch-brackets, etc. The pieces and panels to be carved were cut out and fitted to the waggon, then unscrewed, numbered and sent off to the carver. After the sons took over, the vans tended to become more decorative. They 'flashed them up a bit, curved the lintel over the door, put globe scrolls front and back and an extra 2in to the wheels'.

In World War I both brothers joined the army, making and repairing wheels in France behind the lines, living fairly well while, unknown to them, the family at home had to scrimp. The workshops, in which their sister used to help, closed down 1916-19. Re-starting after the war the brothers would have no truck with motor transport. To make poor trade appear to be good, they placed work-in-progress in full view of passers-by, though when other makers reduced prices they lost many orders because Herbert refused to agree to reductions. Their last Gypsy van was built in about 1926, but they otherwise continued until 1933 when Albert died.— 'He wouldn't have even a motor hearse. He was against the Motor Age.' The workshops, sold in the 1950s, were demolished for building.

Bow-tops that can easily be confused with Wright's were built by other makers. For example, his head man, Uriah Hurst of Woodlesford, continued building after Wright closed down, and his two sons as *Hurst Brothers* built several good ones on lines hardly distinguishable from Wright's. Others that were almost identical were made by *R. W. Hodgson* of Halifax.

With Wright at Rothwell Haigh and Dunton at Reading, *Fred Hill* of Swinefleet, on the Yorkshire-Lincolnshire border, was the best-known builder for Gypsies, noted for his Bow-tops. Like Wright he practised at no great distance from Leeds and typified the best craftsmen in the trade. His eldest son, Rowland, who continued the business until 1966, provided most of our information about it.

A native of Hagnaby, Lincolnshire, Fred Hill was apprenticed as a joiner wheelwright at Alford and, after a short time as journeyman joiner at Derby and Owston Ferry, he set up on his own account at 74 High Street, Swinefleet, in 1894 when he was twenty-five. His capital was £60 and a bag of tools, but he built the business up to a point where it was the largest village wheelwright's and joiner's in Yorkshire, making waggons, carts and lurries, later adding motor caravans and motor-lorry coach building. He was expert as joiner, wheelwright, smith, painter and decorator, and built vans for showmen as well as Gypsies.

When well established he moved along the High Street to Bank House, two acres of land and a big barn. Here he built a spread of workshops that still stand, weedgrown and empty: a large brick structure built 'like a church' with benches all around the walls, for constructing the big waggons; a tiled-roof barn containing blacksmith's shop, metal forge and workshop; a great corrugated iron building with cart and waggon workshop and paint-shop; a shed comprising sawmill and lathe shop; an electric light generator shed; drying sheds

115

for converted timber; and huts with bunks to accommodate visiting Gypsies. Left of the front yard stood the family dwelling house, with lock-up accommodation nearby where the Gypsies could secure their harness, jewellery, china and other personal possessions while the waggons were being repaired. Through the blacksmith's shop in another yard the wheels were hooped, the hooping oven standing against the brick wall of the main workshops and the hooping plate or platform at the yard's centre. Altogether these premises covered half an acre, and made Dunton's at Reading look pathetically cramped.

Fred had illustrations printed on his letter-paper of the two types in which he specialised—the Bow-top and the Ledge. He repaired every sort of waggon, and at some time or other had vans of all the principal builders in his yard. A typical Hill Bow-top, unlike a 'Bill Wright', has a wide bed (floor) with a narrow ledge below the bow, and the wheels running under (see plate page 89). Many 'accommodations' were built, two-wheeled pot carts with canvas tilt on a bowed wood frame with let-down bed attached which could be taken off and set down on the ground like a tent when the owner drove out hawking. He also made four-wheeled drays, spring carts and pot waggons with 'accommodation' tops, though not the elaborate boat-shaped pot waggons that Bill Wright made at Rothwell. Often he had two vans building at a time, and made a dray in two weeks, wheels and all; but a living waggon took the usual time with most builders, six months.

Gypsies were in and out of the yard continually—Smiths, Boswells, Gaskins, Prices, McGuires, Douglases, Squires, Lees, Wests, Calladines. To them parleying was a game; as often as not they would try to twist out of paying the full price, and occasionally there was fighting. For instance, when 'Nosey' Wilson refused the agreed price when the van was finished, 'we got to arguing with him', wrote Fred's son, 'and he lost his temper and swore for fifteen minutes without repeating himself once! He threatened to chop the van up, chop the spokes out, and set fire to it. My father, calm as always, said "Look, Nosey, pay me up. Then we'll lend you the tools to smash it and *give* you the shavings and oil to burn it!" Nosey saw the funny side, paid up and brought two more vans into the yard for repair. Most of the Gypsies liked to trade this way, making a lot of shout but knowing that we made good vans, cheap.'

Two other families, McGuires, were jealous of each other. The one was in the yard awaiting a van when the other arrived; argument led to shouting, then to fighting, a scrap that lasted some time. On another occasion old 'Wisdom' Smith, having had overmuch to drink, bragged that he could jump farther than any of his mates and challenged anyone to beat him for £1. He had several takers and jumped first but only once. He slipped backwards on the loose gravel, cracked his head and couldn't try again. Keeping such customers happy meant that there was more to building waggons than workmanship, but the boss of Bank House was not merely phlegmatic and firm but was 'built like a tank'.

In the 1920s when the demand for horse-drawn vans was fading, Fred built living van bodies onto Ford chassis for Gypsies, and was perhaps the first to do so, thus making forerunners of today's motor-caravans. They were panelled, scrolled, and lined, with lantern roofs, stoves, engraved glass and tasselled blinds. Each vehicle had its name painted in large capitals on the front or crown-board. 'Nellie' and 'Drusilla' were made for the Gray family, Romany carpet salesmen. The firm's last horse-drawn van, an Open-lot with a square bow, was built for 'Deaf' Benny Smith just before Fred died aged 74 years in 1946. His eldest son, Rowland, continued for his mother until she died in 1964, after which he closed down.

Rowland Hill had started as a four-shilling-a-week apprentice in 1910. He normally worked till midnight, perhaps making spokes for a set of wheels: 50 spokes to a set of 48, the two extra in case any were spoiled. Invalided from the army in World War I he concentrated on the painting and, despite a partially disabled right hand, is still, in his seventies, a fast and deft freehand scroll-painter and liner. He gave us a demonstration, including his method of 'dog-bollocking' with a draw-knife (cutting butterfly chamfers), finishing with a light, rounded spokeshave. Today, living in a modern bungalow alongside the weed-grown workshops and yards, he amuses himself making ornamental wheelbarrows and miniature flat carts and still enjoys doing small lettering and embellishing jobs. One of these, not long since, took first prize in the Isle of Man for decorated motor-cycle tanks. At 74 years of age, he bought back his father's original premises and there set up his son in a joinery business. He takes some pride in the perpetuation of a family tradition.

Of such stuff, then, were *vardo* builders made.

118

CONSTRUCTION & EXTERIORS

In this and ensuing chapters we shall consider the technicalities. To do so we must necessarily assume on the reader's part a knowledge of the terminology of the wheelwright and waggon builder (see Sturt, Arnold and Jenkins in the bibliography). In this chapter we shall deal first with construction, materials and exterior equipment generally; then with details pertaining to each type. But as some details are common to all types we shall use the Reading as our base for these.

Two elements are paramount: the underworks ('unders') and the timber. If either is at fault the whole waggon is at risk. The unders were and still are the first consideration when ordering or buying a van; on them depends the owner's living, and even the lives of himself, his family and his horses.

Thoroughly seasoned, 'clean' timber is the second essential. A builder's workmanship may have been excellent but unless he used good timber, accurately milled and free from knots, and carried enough stock to hold it long enough to allow for a second shrinkage after sawing to shape, he could not build a waggon that would last. In practice the best makers would not waste their craftsmanship on poor material. An old Gypsy, calling on Dunton, expected to find finished

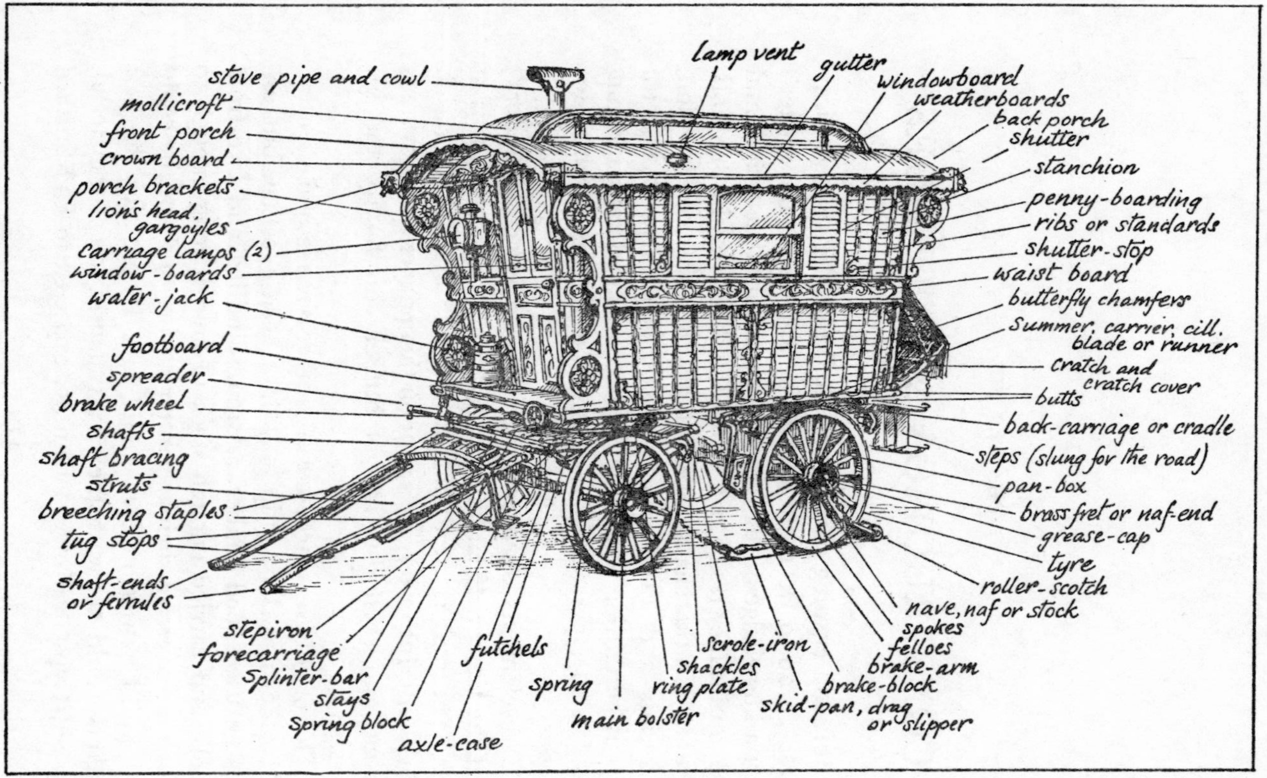

Fig 7

lamp vent

stove pipe and cowl
mollicroft
front porch
crown board
porch brackets
lions head
gargoyles
carriage lamps (2)
window-boards
water jack
footboard
spreader
brake wheel
shafts
shaft-bracing
struts
breeching staples
tug stops
shaft-ends
or females

gutter
windowboard
weatherboards
back porch
shutter
stanchion
penny-boarding
ribs or standards
shutter-stop
waist board
butterfly chamfers
summer, carrier, cill,
blade or runner
cratch and
cratch cover
butts
back-carriage or cradle
steps (slung for the road)
pan-box
brass feet or naf-end
grease-cap
tyre
roller-scotch

nave, naf or stock
spokes
felloes
brake-arm
brake-block
brake-block
skid-pan, drag
or slipper

scrole-iron
shackles
ring plate
main bolster

futchels
spring

step-iron
forecarriage
splinter-bar
stays
spring block
axle-case

the waggon he had ordered some months previously. He was shown several tied-up piles of ribs, framing and match-boards. 'That's your waggon,' said Dunton. The prescribed period for second shrinkage had not yet elapsed. Until it had assembly was unthinkable.

We will now consider the main components (Fig 7).

The under-carriage consists of two parts: fore-carriage or lock, and hind-carriage or cradle. The fore-carriage facilitates steering and comprises an elaborate frame structure of well-seasoned ash to which the shafts are attached. It is fixed under the front bolsters or cross-members beneath the wag-gon by means of a long central king-pin through the two main bolster pieces. This enables the whole fore-carriage with its front wheels to swivel freely on two greased steel rings between. These ring-plates are about $1\frac{1}{2}$in wide by $\frac{1}{4}$in thick and, for stability, should be 3ft 4in or more in circum-ference.

The frame of the fore-carriage below the ring-plates con-sists of parallel ash members (futchels), usually six, arranged lengthways and held together by cross-members notched into their top sides. The central cross-member may be 3in or 4in wide, twice the thickness of the others and matching in weight the main bolster above it upon which rests the body of the waggon. In well-built waggons the futchels are shaped in a shallow S-curve (or swan's neck) which enhances the appearance of the unders. This graceful shaping brings the splinter-bar up towards the level of the ring-plates, distribut-ing the friction on the turntable more evenly against the pull on the shafts. The futchels project forward under the footboard and are fixed together by the ash splinter-bar, to which the shafts are attached by means of barrel-eye hinge bolts and a steel draw-bar or draft pin. The splinter-bar is attached either by mortising flush onto the fore ends of the

121

Nearside rear corner structure

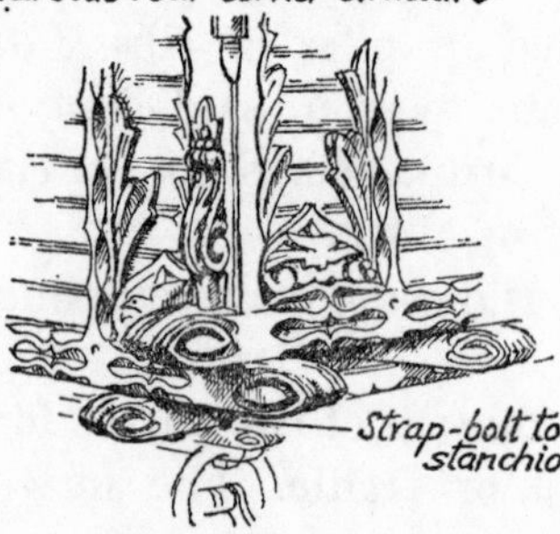

Strap-bolt to stanchion

Fig 8

futchels or, more elaborately, by being lap-jointed to the tops of the futchels about 1½in back, the projecting butts being chamfered or carved in fiddle-heads. A top-mounted splinter-bar is kept from tilting forward by six metal stays from the topside to the next cross-member on the lock frame. All lap-joints on the framing are bolted together.

The front suspension of the waggon is effected between the framing and the axle-case. To the underside of the outer futchels are bolted the scrole-irons, by means of which the whole structure is hung on the springs (Fig 9). Springs are long for easy riding and consist of seven to ten leaves of $\frac{5}{16}$in steel, jack-bolted at the fore-end and shackled to the scrole-irons behind. These springs are bolted through the axle blocks into the elm axle-case, the whole being securely clamped together by a pair of stout staple-bolts and plates.

On hills an additional horse (a 'sider') is sometimes required to pull beside the shaft horse. To facilitate this an accessory called a spreader can be linked to a ring-bolt beneath the off-side summer (Fig 5).

The hind-carriage, not concerned with steering, is simpler. It normally consists of two cross-members, spaced about 4ft apart, bolted to the summers of the waggon bed. Beneath these, about 2in in from the sides of the waggon, are bolted two longitudinal chamfered members to which the spring scrole-irons are bolted. For his elegant Bow-tops, Wright employed two pairs of light cross-members about 9in apart in place of the usual, stout, single ones. All projecting butts on the undercarriage and body are either chamfered or carved into fiddle-heads or gryphon-heads (Fig 24).

Springs and scroles: scrole-irons on Readings and Burtons are normally of the globe kind with the springs attached via the shackles, 'eyes up'. Lighter waggons such as Bow-tops and Ledges have bridge or swan's-neck scroles, the spring ends curved over, 'eyes down' (Fig 9).

Wheels: elegance of wheel, achieved by size and proportion, characterises the best vans. Within reasonable limits the larger the wheel the easier it will roll. Pulling over uneven

Scrole-irons:

Back Side
'Globe'

'Bridge'

'Swan's-neck'

'Dumb-jack'

Fig 9

or soft ground calls for a wide diameter wheel but weight must be considered against this. Wheel spokes are of oak and the felloes of the rim of ash, both heavy timbers, and additional is the weight of the iron tyres. The best builders struck a nice balance between strength, weight and functional elegance.

The wheel-hubs, stocks or naves, are of elm, a hardwood with a devious grain of interwoven fibres which make serious splitting unlikely; the turned and hollowed stocks are bonded with iron nave-bands, or stock-hoops, shrunk or sweated on, as are the tyres.

The rim of the wheel comprises a ring of segments, the felloes ('fellies'), one to every two spokes, and these are of well-seasoned ash. There is no standard number of spokes but it is always even. Most vans have twelve in the front wheel and fourteen in the rear, the ratio in smaller vans being ten and twelve. Spokes are of flawless English oak and, according to Hill, ideally selected so that the backs are of heart-of-oak for strength, the sapwood being towards the face of the wheel. They are tenoned into the stock in a staggered line for added rigidity, and at a slight angle outwards so that the wheel is dished. The dish is important to counter the constant knocking outwards of the greased axle shoulder against the stock as the horse pulls along the road. Warner hubs with iron casing fitted over the stocks to hold the spokes were never used on Gypsy caravans. Tyres are of 2-2$\frac{1}{2}$in by $\frac{3}{4}$in-thick iron, with a round edge to the outside projecting $\frac{1}{4}$in to protect the painted surface of the wheel from scraping against bank or curb. The best vans have brass bell-mouthed

Brass Wheel Frets (in section)

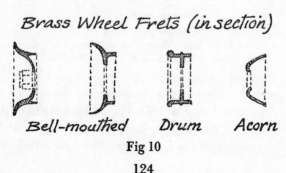

Bell-mouthed   Drum   Acorn

Fig 10

Page 125 (above) Brush waggon at Chatteris Fen before 1914;
(below) first of the three kinds of Burton waggon described in
Chapter 6, this one Dunton-built

Page 126 (above) Second of the three kinds of Burton described in Chapter 6, this one by Watts of Bridgwater; (below) the third kind of Burton (this by Wheeler) described in Chapter 6

frets or 'naf-ends' on the hubs. Many of the later waggons have these chromium-plated, to minimise the need to polish, but none look so well as polished brass (Fig 10).

Axles are drabble type, made by firms that specialised in them. Builders would ask whether the customer wanted London or Yorkshire drabble. Wright usually used Yorkshire drabble. Drabble axles were made separately for each wheel, the short axle arm being fitted into the underside of the wooden axle-case, secured by a clip on the outside and a staple-bolt and plate on the inside (Fig 11). This was standard wheelwright practice for farm carts and waggons. When Dunton used London drabble he shut on a connecting piece of square section iron so that the axle arms on each side were connected, let into the underside of the arched axle-case and secured with bolts and plates. He bought his London drabbles from Isaiah Oldbury of Wednesbury, Staffordshire, his Yorkshire from Kendrick of Leeds, who also supplied Wright, Hill and others. The axle spindle of fine-turned steel fits into the 'box', which is a steel tube tapered to fit the axle arm and is wedged snugly into the elm stock. Wheels are secured to the axle arm either by a linch-pin and washer (Yorkshire drabble) or by two counter-threaded nuts (London drabble). A brass grease-cap, usually bearing the builder's name and locality, closes the wheel hub against dirt and weather.

Shafts, variously referred to by travellers as 'sharps', 'sharves' or 'rods', are hinged to the splinter-bar (the front cross-member of the lock) by adjacent pairs of barrel-eye ring-bolts through which the draw-bar is passed and secured by a split pin or 'feather'. If this attachment broke, swinging the van around suddenly in the road, a bad accident could easily occur; and consequently some travellers insisted on three ring-bolts instead of two. But more than a pair, each

127

H

firmly secured through the framing of both shafts and fore-carriage, is rare.

Shafts are of English ash, 2in deep with a lateral S-curve, tapered for lightness along the length towards the points, the wood at its thickest at the point of maximum stress. Weight is also minimised by narrowing the top face with a draw-knife. The framing at the base of the shafts is reinforced by iron straps bolted through the timber. Some good vans have S-curved timber supports inside the shafts, reinforced by a 'top bracket iron' or strap bolted through; but simpler shafts are strengthened by diagonal iron stays bolted across the inside angle between shafts and frame. Butterfly chamfers on the shaft framing match those on the fore-carriage; apart from being decorative, these are again functional in that they cut down weight without significantly lessening strength.

Shaft ends are tipped with brass ferrules. As a speciality, they have leather shrunk around the ends, down to a point beyond the tug stops, and another band around at the point where the breeching strap is buckled through the staples. The purpose of this is to protect the paint and timber from the constant chafing of the straps, tugs and collar. On traps and carriages 'for the gentry' this was common practice, but some travellers would not have it, as the leather tended to soften and stretch away from the wood in wet weather. Where leather is not used these areas are painted a dark colour toning with the general decor.

Struts are provided on most shafts, fastened with eye-bolts to the underside. They were strapped back out of the way after the horse was backed into the shafts. Some travellers believed struts to be a nuisance as, from the side of the waggon, they caused them to have to go around the raised shafts to ascend the steps, though on the near side it is of course possible to take a short cut by way of the step-iron. Struts could be an advantage in that they obviated the need for steps at all, and shafts propped on their struts in the raised position could serve as useful rails for airing the *copples* (bedclothes), for beating the carpet or hanging up the harness.

The roof is proofed, and in its construction the purpose of the moulding on the outer side of its weatherboards is to batten down the proofing material. In building, the roof is

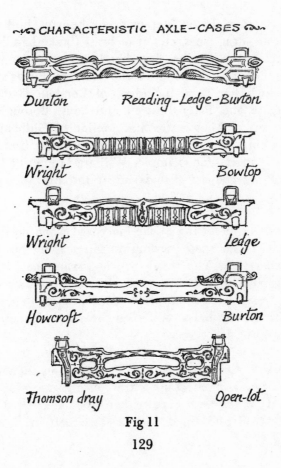

~◌ CHARACTERISTIC AXLE-CASES ◌~

Durton   Reading-Ledge-Burton

Wright   Bowtop

Wright   Ledge

Howcroft   Burton

Thomson dray   Open-lot

Fig 11

129

painted before the moulding is finally fixed in position. While the paint is still tacky a sheet of fine white linen is laid and fastened down over it on the outside of the weather-boards. This is then painted, and another sheet laid over it, a process repeated several times. Finally, the moulding is screwed or nailed onto the weatherboards to hold the proof-ing in position.

EXTERIOR FITTINGS

These, whether of iron (step-irons, brake-arms, brake-screws, scrole-irons, drag-shoes, etc) or of brass (brake handles, shaft ends, frets, grab handles, door handles, etc)—were supplied by manufacturers catering for the builders. Firms specialis-ing in such hardware included, in London, Gadstone of Bishopsgate and Peter Boswell and Sons, Borough Road; also Leeson of Manchester and Mellor of Oldham. Often builders obtained their fittings from specialist ironmongers in their district—for example, William Haines of Reading who did his country rounds of smiths and wheelwrights regularly.

Step-irons, for mounting to the footboard when on the road, are bolted to the shaft framing on the nearside and usually have two treads. The treads are in various patterns, shut onto the arm to order. Among Gypsies horseshoe-and-frog pattern treads were often preferred. The best step-irons are embellished with brass 'swells' on the shank to match those on the splinter-bar stays.

Brakes are always screw-pattern, operating on the two hind wheels from a brass crank-wheel on the nearside of the footboard. Brake-blocks are of hardwood decorated with a painted scroll and lined with a fibre belt or, latterly, a section of motorcar tyre with the nails recessed between the treads. Brake-arms, not to be weakened by turned swells, are decorated by a band of sheet brass embossed above and below.

Handles: grab-handles are fixed to the jambs on either side of the door, necessary for steadying oneself when rising from the footboard while on the road. The best are brass-mounted with wine-coloured, cut glass grips. The pan-box doors have matching handles of smaller size.

Lamps: brass or plated carriage-lamp brackets are screwed to the ribs on either side of the door above the waistboard. Carriage lamps are brass-mounted with spring-fed candles and silver-plated interior reflectors. Lamps with a horse-shoe-shape reflector cowl were often preferred by Gypsies.

Other equipment with a good waggon as it issued from the builder's yard could include:

Sun-sheets of cotton duck. On the pitch they were draped around the waggon from hooks atop the weatherboards, reaching the ground on all four sides and dividing into two curtains in front. Paintwork suffers more from exposure to the heat of the sun than from any other weathering cause. The sun-sheets are absorbent, not proofed, and travellers stopping for long on one pitch in winter would sometimes put them up to cut down condensation in the van.

A light narrow ladder was often carried between the floor runners, and was for such purposes as pulling out the chimney for cleaning or to avoid its being *pogered* by overhanging branches, low bridges, etc.

A hooked pole, like a long shepherd's crook, was carried for pulling dead branches out of trees for the *yog*. Like the ladder, it ran the length of the van and slid in under the floor from the rear to rest on the under-carriage cross-members.

THE READING

Measurements: Usually 10ft long with the front porch projecting a further 18in and the back porch 14in. Some vans are 6in longer in the body. The walls lean out 4in all around towards the eaves. Relative measurements of vans made to the same design by the same builder vary slightly although, usually, not significantly. Hill cut templates for curves and reverses but seldom, if ever, kept them for re-use. Measurements and curves were varied to make the best use of the timber in stock. A fully equipped ten-footer weighs about 30cwt.

Underworks: wheels are 5ft diameter at back and 3ft 6in in front, the floor or bed riding 4ft 3in from the road.

Timber: most of the body construction is of straight-grained pine for lightness of weight, but most builders made the bottom frame or 'bed-piece' of oak. (To this Dunton was an exception. Believing that a softwood should not be tenoned into a hardwood, he compromised by making the front and rear burgins of oak but the summers of red deal like the ribs, cutting down on weight at the same time). The carved facia on the footboard is also of oak to resist knocks and kicks. Curved pieces in the body construction, such as the arched door lintel, are of ash for toughness. Carved porch brackets are of sycamore or mahogany. Interior in-built furniture is of red pine free of knots, stained, grained or scumbled, or, if the customer could afford it, of french-polished mahogany. Where pine was used, the bowed pieces in the front of cupboards and chests of drawers were fashioned from ash to provide strength on the cross-grain.

A design flaw: Dunton's Reading has one structural defect that became evident only after long use and was never resolved. This is the tendency for the van to arch its back slightly due to the accent at the front end of weight on the footboard by day and at the rear end on the bed by night. This fault, caused by stress over a long period, might have been alleviated had the builder placed the fore-carriage slightly further forward under the footboard. But this kind of defect takes a long time to show itself, longer still to be recognised and remedied without creating new problems.

Curved members: their use does much for a waggon's appearance and usually has a practical purpose. The graceful S-line of the steps, like the already-mentioned swan's neck curve on the fore-carriage, has a function: to enable the steps to clear the shaft framing when the shafts are strutted in the raised position on the pitch. Dunton, however, did go out of his way to add grace to the appearance of his waggons. The arching and side-winding of the butterfly-chamfered cross-members on a Dunton fore-carriage have to be seen to be appreciated; neither drawing nor photograph can do full justice to them.

The body is always of beaded match-boarding, tongue-and-groove or sometimes lapped, supported on the outside by upright chamfered ribs. Narrow match-boarding, called penny-board (being roughly a penny's width), was perhaps the most sought after; but often used was penny-farthing board, a wider and therefore cheaper product. When penny-farthing or wider boards were used for the walls, penny-

Fig 12 *Dunton coachwork showing chamfering on sills and standards, beaded penny-boarding, and typical inter-rib carving*

boards would still be used for the roof, which requires the narrower board to enable it to follow the curve of the arch. Although the practical superiority of penny-boarding over the wider kind is debateable, the narrower board with its double beading is richer and more decorative.

Ribs: the upright ribs, or standards, are properly chamfered from top to bottom (Fig 12) although the earlier vans, and later ones of more modest build, are 'long-chamfered', given one long bevel each side, the draw-knife finishing about 3in from the mortised joints. The original purpose of chamfering was to lighten the structure and add finish; but the later combination of single and butterfly chamfers, gilded or painted in different colours and lined out, does much to enhance appearance. The best builders mortised the ribs

134

right through to the underside of the summers, optimising strength and reducing the likelihood of trapping moisture.

Weatherboards along the eaves and over the porches are scalloped. Of the side ones the top serves to form gutters along the roof, the bottom forming a shutter slide. Similarly, scalloped boards are fixed around the middle of the body immediately below the windows and form the bottom slide for the shutters. Lighter scalloped weatherboards run along the top edges of the skylight. All these boards carry a half-round chip-carved moulding.

Skylights: early Readings have an arched roof with no clerestory skylight. When the first mollicroft roofs were built around 1900 they were introduced for showmen. At first they did not appeal to the Gypsies, accustomed as they were to the half light of a bender tent or a Bow-top; also when the lamp was lit at night a roof-light signalled their presence in a lane or against a wood.

The skylight curves up from a point over the front and rear walls to a height usually of about 10in, although Dunton's are slightly lower. In frontal elevation they have a $1\frac{1}{2}$in rise in the centre, curving laterally to shed water. Readings by Wright have a straight fall to the skylight fore and aft, as do his Ledges and most early Burtons; but the curved ends are better looking and, while on the move, are rather more effective in fending off overhanging branches (Fig 4 page 50).

Skylights on each side have four long panes of patterned, frosted glass, the end ones opening on a pivot in the centre. The angle pieces formed where the skylight curves down to meet the roof are fitted with coloured glass, usually red. Readings built before the introduction of the skylight, the so-called kite waggons, have side walls on average 3in higher than was later found necessary.

Roof rails: roofs of some earlier vans without skylight have light iron rails fixed around the edge for stowing baskets, rugs and other goods for sale but such racks were not much required by Romanies (see plate page 125).

The door of the Reading, indeed of the Ledge and the Bow-top, opens outwards; those on all vans for showmen, even the one-horse Burton sometimes used by Gypsies, open inwards. The two hinged windows above the door, fitting the curved lintel, also open outwards on a Reading and are hooked back to the front wall of the waggon.

Windows, side and back, in the early waggons are made in two hinged panels opening outwards to conserve space, and care had to be taken to close them before pulling off the pitch. Somewhere around 1890 builders started fitting light sash windows complete with pulley-wheel, cord and weights recessed in the jambs, and a central brass-mounted 'window-silencer' for locking shut. Sash windows usually have a narrow border pane of patterned, frosted glass and small square corner panes of red glass cut on the inside with a white star or flower. This tended to give way to a single pane when interior carved window-boards came into use but some Gypsies seem to have wanted the best of both.

Shutters, to side and rear windows, and of the sliding type, are usually louvred Venetian style with chamfered frames and scalloped slats, but some have panel shutters relief-carved, painted and gilded (see plate page 54). Each shutter has one or two pairs of knobs, early ones of white china, superseded by wine-coloured cut glass in the 1900s. Carved stops on the waistboard prevent the shutters sliding away from the windows. Two early photographs show windows in the front crown-board, over the door, but old Gypsies say this was unusual; for most the crown-board scroll was the centrepiece of the waggon's decoration (Fig 22 page 174).

Carving of crown-boards, doors, porch-brackets, gargoyles, etc, is characteristic of the Reading, and is dealt with in Chapter Eight.

THE LEDGE

Measurements: the usual body length is 9ft 6in to 10ft. The size of porches and footboard is similar to that of a Reading. The floor or bed has a width of 4ft 2in to 4ft 6in, with walls below the ledges usually vertical but occasionally with an outward slope matching that above the ledge. The walls below the ledge are 18in high and the ledges built out 8in over the wheels. Above the ledges the walls slope out 2in to a width similar to that of the Reading. These measurements are approximate, as they vary from builder to builder and even from van to van from the same yard. The weight of a 10ft Ledge ex works was 25-28cwt, although the 10ft 6in Dunton Ledge illustrated in the scale drawings is about 30cwt.

Underworks are similar in proportion to those of a Reading, though on the whole smaller, the large hind wheels measuring about 4ft 8in like the other Ledge-built type, the Bow-top. Axle-cases are usually lathe-turned—a style favoured by Midlands builders for Gypsy customers. Turned axles, sometimes mounted by elaborate bridged extensions of the spring blocks, are a feature of both Ledges and Bow-tops and became so closely identified with the Gypsies that no showman would have a turned axle case on his waggon.

Porch-brackets: next to the overall structure, their style is the most important characteristic of this type (Fig 23 page 175).

137

Fig 13

They are commonly formed by the match-boarding of the side walls projecting fore and aft and cut to the required shape (Fig 13). The ends of the penny-boards are separately shaped, like feathers on a wing, chamfered and tipped with gold leaf (Chapter Eight). They are strengthened by a thin Y-shaped brace or strap of iron screwed through to each board, from which travellers occasionally called them 'strap waggons'. Wright and Hill, well known for their Ledge vans, always made them with these match-board brackets, but some others, notably Dunton and Jones, fixed separate, carved porch-brackets as on a Reading.

Walls: ribs, waistboards, weatherboards, moulding, roof, etc, are similar in design to the Reading, but the construction of the side walls below the ledges is often rib-and-panel instead of rib-and-matchboard. These rectangular, flat panels are of mahogany embellished in the manner stated in Chapter Eight.

138

Ledge scrolls: Ledge waggons are strutted with S-shaped brass supports that rest on the projecting fiddle-headed burgins of the bottom frame and again in the centre on the front projecting cross-piece of the cradle. The central brass support is sometimes supplemented by secondary scrolling brass brackets on either side of it. This is particularly functional on the off-side where, inside the van at this point, the ledge forms a seat long enough to accommodate two hefty people.

Spindle racks: another characteristic shared with the Bow-top is the inclusion of turned spindle racks about 2ft 3in long from floor level up, to join the ledge in the space over the front wheels (see plate page 72). These are sometimes bow-fronted, sometimes straight, and they have a small spindle door in the centre. They were used for stowing vegetables or other things needed on the road or for keeping bantams, chickens or other small livestock out of harm's way. Occasionally a van was built with a boxed-out fireplace over the front wheel on the offside and a corresponding cupboard on the nearside, taking up the space normally used for the spindle racks. Though this allowed for more space inside, it looked clumsy.

Doors are of course always at the front and normally central but on the Ledge and the Bow-top, both of which have ledges, the door is occasionally set off-centre and towards the near-side, ostensibly to facilitate accommodation of the stove.

THE BOW-TOP

Measurements: Bow-tops by Wright and Hill vary in body length from 9ft 6in to 10ft 4in. The type is light in weight. Albert Wright wrote to a prospective customer in the early 1920s: 'Most of our Bow-top vans is just under a 1 ton but if you come over and take some of the fitting off it would be Lighter...'

Underworks: the back wheels are approximately 4ft 8in and the front 3ft 4in. The structure of the unders is similar to that of the Ledge although rather lighter, Wright going to the trouble of tapering all members of the under-carriage for maximum lightness and economy of structure compatible with function. Scrole-irons on a Wright waggon are usually either bridge or swan's-neck, with the spring 'eyes-down'. Also, the van being lighter, his wheels have fellies shallower than most, $2\frac{1}{4} \times 2\frac{1}{4}$in, an aid to elegance overall.

Porches: in Wright Bow-tops these project 14in at the top of the curve, cutting back to 9in at the ledges at both ends, giving a nice raking angle to the bow. The front and back walls are vertical. Porches are match-boarded all around inside to protect the canvas from weather and wear.

Bow structure: the hoops of the bow, of $2\frac{1}{2} \times \frac{3}{4}$in bent ash, are usually eight in number and spaced about 14in apart. They are jointed at the bottom into the ledges and connected by seven horizontal laths to make a rigid frame. Inside these, matchboard walls rise from the ledges to just above elbow height. Over the hooped frame is stretched a patterned and piled carpet material, or patterned felt, and outside this the green proofed canvas. Bow-tops were never built with side windows, although these—and even a skylight—were occasionally added later.

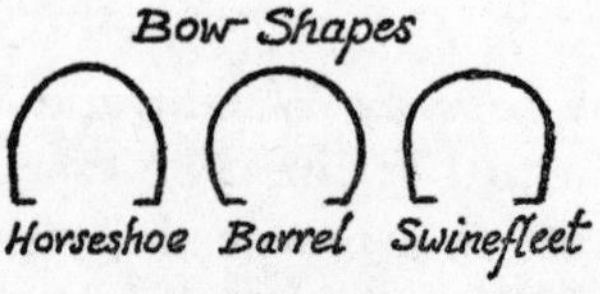

Bow Shapes

Horseshoe   Barrel   Swinefleet

Fig 14

Weatherboards: the canvas is battened down over the front and back porches by the bowed weatherboard which, in early Wright waggons, is fret-carved on the inside with 'thumb-ends' tipped with gold, and chamfered on the outside of the curve. On later vans from this and other builders these weatherboards were modified, having shallow-cut chamfered scallops on the inside of the curve and a carved moulding running around the bow. The canvas at the side is fixed down to the outside of the ledges by a weatherboard chamfered top and bottom, usually without any projecting moulding.

Doors and quarter-lights above are stoutly built with deep-chamfered frames and of course opened outwards, Gypsy style. In about 1910 when Bill Wright's sons took over the business, an arched lintel came in, giving the doorway about 3in more headroom, and the crown-board carving was modified accordingly. However the firm continued to build straight lintels occasionally (see plate page 90).

Front waistboards either side of the door are scalloped and beaded, but there was no fixed practice, some vans having them, some not.

THE BRUSH

If any example of this type has survived we have not yet encountered it, and consequently are unable to state measurements. We understand that, fully loaded, it weighed 35-40cwt. Clad with its wares, it must have been a formidable obstacle in a narrow country lane or on a dyked fenland road. The broad characteristics are stated in Chapter Four. (See plate pages 108 and 125).

Some were as well constructed as the best of other types, but they carried no carving. Most were of plain workaday build, sometimes with sloping shelves around the roof instead of iron rails for wicker chairs, and hooks along the sides for other merchandise. The following features are described by Huth.

Underworks: wheels and under-carriage are not dissimilar from those of the preceding types built for Gypsies.

Steps are fixed like those of the old horse-drawn charabanc and, with the half-door, are at the back. Each side they have a hand-rail, the top of which is fixed to the back of the waggon and the bottom to the lowest tread of the steps to act as their support.

Windows: sometimes there is a window at the front similar to the back window of other types, but there are no shutters and sometimes no window at all in front. Each side has one window, also shutterless.

Racks and cases: either side of the door are two racks, one above the other, the uppermost with turned spindles but sometimes made as a glazed cupboard. The lower rack is usually panelled with a narrow spindle rail around its top. Used for the stowage of coconut mats, rugs and large broomheads, these racks stand out flush with the footboard, and between them are turned pillars ascending to the overhanging porch. Brooms with handles were usually hung around the waggon or the handles held in sockets.

The front racks, cases and turned pillars are similar to those at the back. Beneath each side window is a case for such wares as hair-brushes, combs and hand mirrors. This case, with glazed doors and shelves, comes down to the level of the bottom brush rack, with which it stands out flush. As at the back, on each side there are two rows of racks one above the

Page 143 (above) Open-lot built on a Lambert dray, decorated by Jim Berry; (below) typical Open-lot interior and frontal decoration

Page 144 (above) Waggon decoration by Jim Berry; (below) free-hand scrolling on steps, by the same painter

other with turned pillars between them ascending to the overhanging roof. These side racks are much narrower and shallower, being only 6in high; they run the length of the waggon, from the front to the window and glass case, and are continued from the other side of the window to the back of the van. The bottom racks, about 1ft from the sills and curved up over the back wheels to allow clearance space there, were used for the rougher sorts of brush, the varnished and polished kinds being displayed in the glass cases.

Equipment included a light ladder hung at the rear, used for hauling down goods from the higher racks. At the day's end a waterproof sheet, called a 'rounding cloth', was draped around the waggon, an opening left at the rear for access. The wickerwork wares were usually removed from the roof to the ground and covered with another waterproof cloth.

THE BURTON

Measurements: usually the length is 10ft or 10ft 6in, with porches a little shorter than those of the Reading and Ledge. The sides slope out no more than 2in, the usual width being 6ft at the bottom and 6ft 4in at the eaves. Some vans appear as almost rectangular from a low eye level. The weight varies from about 27 to 32cwt.

Underworks: while the front wheels are of much the same height as those already described, about 3ft 4-6in, the back wheels are necessarily closer to them in size, being only 3ft 10in to 4ft high so as to run under the body, where they are set back just inside the bottom sills. Axle-cases are usually straight, square and chamfered like the big, heavily built showmen's waggons, though Dunton's are an exception, his axle-cases being generally arched, a design he used on all

145

J

types. Builders of Burtons and other waggons for showmen in south-eastern England often obtained their unders from F. J. Thomas, of Chertsey, Surrey. It was common for showmen, when ordering from a builder, to stipulate 'Thomas's' or 'Chertsey' unders.

The roof has an arch flatter than those of other types. It always has gutters and a skylight usually broader and a little taller than that of a Reading. The skylight first made its appearance on Burtons for showmen, and the earlier ones have vertical, square ends and run the full length of the roof, the portion over-running the porches used as stowage space. In later vans these butt-ends are streamlined like those on the old Pullman railway cars. By the early 1900s Gypsies had skylights incorporated in their waggons; they were seldom carried over the porches but curved up from the point above the crown-board. This kind of skylight, the mollicroft, was distinct from the Pullman, which continued to be built on Burton sub-type (3) described below.

Weatherboards around the eaves are commonly one piece of deep moulding elaborately chip-carved and gilded or sometimes of simple ogee-and-fillet section. Burton weatherboards are rarely scalloped and beaded.

Windows: two per side, complete with shutters, are a characteristic of Burtons, plus one at the rear. This calls for the different interior arrangement described in Chapter seven. Occasionally the offside has no windows at all, presumably because of a tendency for showmen to pull up side by side on the *tober* or against a hedge or building. When blind, the off-side has dummy shutters to balance the sides' appearance.

146

Basic shape: although this is always straight-sided with wheels running under the body, there are three variants of the Burton: Sub-type (1) is the most common, of panel construction all around with elaborately carved oak plaques fixed to each panel (see plate page 125). Orton, Howcroft and Dunton made vans of this kind. The lower cost ones have panels decorated with painted scrolls and flowers. Sub-type (2) as built by Watts of Bridgwater, Somerset, has a panelled and carved front but rib-and-matchboard sides and back, with waist panels about 7in deep, mounted with carving, running around the body below the windows (see plate page 126). Sub-type (3) rib-and-matchboard all around and only one window a side, like the Reading (see plate page 126). This similarity in bodywork causes it sometimes to be mistaken for a Reading, but the decisive feature of the Burton is its upright shape with wheels running under. Leonard of Soham, near Newmarket, was noted for this kind.

Porch-brackets: most Burtons have single brackets under the eaves fore and aft and none on the footboard. These with double porch-brackets in front, typical of the Reading, are comparatively few in number.

Stanchion-jacks were often used by showmen to support a parked waggon at each corner. They steadied it and lifted some of the weight off the unders; but care had to be taken not to jack them too high and unduly stress the body structure.

Sun awning: the front porch was often fitted with a striped canvas awning attached under the porch and strutted from the front corner pillars. These tended to deteriorate after a few years and were seldom replaced.

147

THE OPEN-LOT

Measurements are about 9ft 3in long by 5ft 2in wide. The weight is light at about 15cwt.

Underworks: evolved from about 1930 and still built, this type has side walls, ledges, back and bowed tilt built onto an existing tradesman's cart, dray, trolley, lurry or bogey, which might be called on to carry up to two tons of scrap metal. The underworks have a supplementary cross-spring over the back axle-case. Unlike Wright's pot carts, drays are fitted with a screw brake similar to that of a living van, operating from a chromium-plated wheel bracketed below the front shutlock. Some of the most suitable were made at Bradford (by Lambert and by Parkinson), at Wakefield (by Wittaker and Hutchins), at Halifax (by Hodgson), and at Falkirk, Scotland (by Thomson). Lambert's drays are particularly well designed, the best having two-way tapered futchels on the lock, fiddle-headed butts and turned axle-cases (see plate page 143).

The shafts are curved both in elevation and plan. On a dray the frame of the fore-carriage and therefore the shaft attachment is at a low level. The shafts are curved up and over to bring them to the required height for harnessing.

Tops: the floor or bed rides about 3ft 4in from the ground, and on this the side walls are fixed with iron brackets on the inside. Walls are usually of pirana pine, about 1ft 3in high, the ends projecting at a raking angle fore and aft to support the porches. These side walls as well as the other panels are vehicles for some magnificent curlicue scroll-painting and lining, with shadowing and gold leaf (see Chapter Eight). Ledges are 10in wide but overhang the side walls by only

3 or 4in, the rest projecting inwards to form narrow seats inside the van.

Bows vary in shape from horseshoe, or a slightly parabolic curve, to a wide bow slightly flattened, called a 'Swinefleet top' after the Bow-tops of this shape built by Hill of that place (Fig 14). A compass curve on a bow is not the best-looking shape but is much improved if made with raking porches as on the best Open-lots.

The rear has a pan-box, chamfered and decorated with scrolls and horses' heads, slung below the covered cratch. The rear window has louvred shutters. In the past few years a further development has emerged, derived from motor trailers: a bay window built out at the rear. This dispenses with the attractive shutters, but more than compensates by adding space, providing a shelf by the bed for a cup of tea or a display of Crown Derby.

Cross-section facing rear

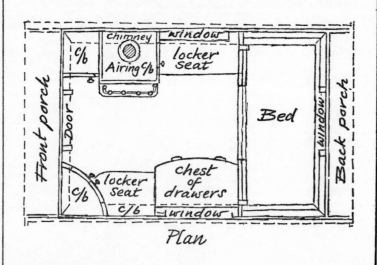

Plan

Fig 15

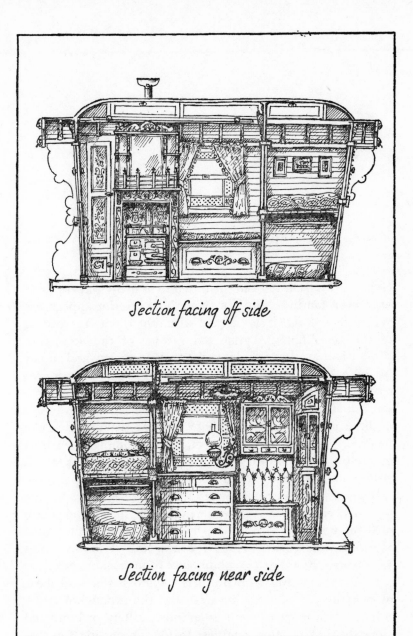

Section facing off side

Section facing near side

Fig 16

CHAPTER SEVEN

INTERIOR FITTINGS AND
FURNISHINGS

Gypsy caravans have been furnished in as many ways as there have been families living in them. The interior appearance varies (though much less so than with other homes) according to the taste, housekeeping and income of the occupants. Limitations are imposed by various considerations and largely by space, for an entire home is contained in a gross floor area that the suburbanite considers the barest minimum for a kitchen alone. The *vardo* does not have even the advantage of the economies made possible by the space-saving fabric of a motorised caravan or a trailer yet, though comprised entirely of pre-twentieth century materials, it does not look at all clumsy or awkward, indeed the reverse (see plate page 53).

The *vardo* builder and his customers achieved elegance empirically, not by the spaciousness inherent in large expanses of floor, wall and ceiling, but by their very opposite. Rich showmen who commissioned the building of massive vans with several rooms and an abundance of mahogany may have provided themselves with prosperity symbols that had more of everything, but it was invariably at the expense of gracefulness. Such waggons were either 'horse killers' or lumbered along behind traction engines. Inside, or outside for that matter, they had little in common with the one-horse *vardo*, in which smallness of scale was imposed by the traveller's way of life. Within that scale it is doubtful whether such high standards, aesthetic and functional, were ever otherwise reached. Few people who have lived in a *vardo* look back on the experience with anything but pleasure. The tiny house composed of the fewest conveniences and possessions can be every bit as civilised and charming as the Palladian mansion and, for some, more so.

Whether it was realised or not, the interior of the Gypsy caravan pointed the way for the twentieth-century trailer builders, who had all the advantages of modern light-weight materials, many of which, like such substances as ply-wood and aluminium, received impetus from the needs of World War I. Horse-drawn vans have been 'restored' and furnished with means that are essentially products of the twentieth century, though rarely by travellers themselves. Some of them may have a functional advantage but the overall effect, practically and aesthetically, is invariably depressing.

Perhaps because Gypsies generally are conservative and traditionalist by nature, their taste and style are normally fifty years behind the *gaujo's*—a fact that has trapped people into dating old vans earlier than in truth they are. Fashion in our time has for everyone become more and more fluid, less and less crystallized, under the influence of wealth more widely shared, of the popular press, the cinema, television and travel-for-all. And Gypsy appearances have been an exception to this only in that their rate of change is slower. Even in their modern trailers the travellers stick to their old tastes—the Crown Derby, the lace, the family photographs in silver frames. The few that yet travel the roads in a horse-drawn waggon, a Bow-top or an Open-lot, do so because they like the old ways best; they are perhaps the equivalent of the *gaujo* families who prefer a period house furnished with the

Chippendale or Hepplewhite of another age. Even the Open-lots that post-date World War I have the quality of the day when Horse was King of the Road, much as 'Georgian' villas are furnished with Victoriana and 'repros', but with this important difference—that while a house of any date may be furnished without offence to taste with things that obviously post-date its time of building, a horse-drawn home-on-wheels demands the impedimenta of the period to 'look right'. A *vardo* decorated and furnished out of the essential period that is its charm is a mongrel-like anachronism, even if its use in life has sunk to the level of a changing room beside a private swimming pool.

Limitations of space, its essential period, and the taste of the people for whom it was built, then, narrow down severely the degree to which one Gypsy caravan interior differs in appearance from another. But in describing the interior, its furnishings and fittings, we do not wish to imply that these are necessarily so; only that they typify the best as originally built and equipped. Old vans that survive, like houses, have all undergone changes.

LAYOUT

As all furniture is in-built, layout is the decisive consideration in a van's interior. The normal layout, evolved in the second half of the nineteenth century, is outlined briefly in Chapter Four and is perhaps more readily apparent from our illustrations. To it there are three exceptions. In the inside of a Brush waggon, as its door was peculiarly located at the rear, the layout was more or less the simple reverse of other types. Also the Burton, with its two windows either side instead of the usual one (see plate pages 125 and 126), has its stove centred between the windows at the left as one enters; opposite, similarly placed, is the chest of drawers with table top, above which is usually a shallow, glazed cupboard for table-ware with small drawers beneath for cutlery.

The third exception is the Open-lot which, despite being the smallest type, has the illusion internally of being larger (see plate page 143 and Figs 19 and 20). Its stove is not boxed-in and is small in size; also it has no locker seats but only extensions of the ledges. The chest of drawers is not so deep, and its bed-place is identical to the Bow-top's (described later), complete with drawers but without the pull-out slotted table. In the corners on either side of the door, and resting on the ledges, is a tall cupboard of two compartments, one above the other. The upper one is tall and has a glazed door, the lower small with a square-panelled door. The frames are deep-chamfered, gilded and fine-lined.

In all types other than these variations of layout are exceptional and uncharacteristic.

CEILINGS AND WINDOWS

The underside of the bow of the Bow-top (Figs 17 and 18) was at one time of patterned pile carpeting but in the 1920s and 1930s felting became more common. Hill used a compact felt, red in colour with black scroll designs and, later, a cream with a pattern such as grapes-and-leaves printed in one colour, red or brown. The Open-lot is lined with a printed fabric, usually flowers on a light ground, beneath an insulating layer of under-felt.

Of the other types the pine ceiling is of course the under-side of the penny-boarding roof with its vaulted, chamfered ribs. The boards are grained or scumbled, and the ribs usually painted, gilded and fine-lined like those on the out-side of the waggon. Burton roofs are sometimes panelled over the ribs, giving the roof a double skin, insulating it and reducing condensation.

The ceiling of the clerestory skylight, mollicroft or Pull-man, is usually panelled below the match-boarding with the framework of the panels grained and fine-lined; the panels themselves painted sky-blue and decorated with gold leaf scrolls and lining. Running the length of the skylight and on either side of it are brass hand-rails, screwed just below the window lights to the main longitudinal members.

Each window has at its foot a removable board, 9in high, to ensure privacy without unduly reducing the entry of daylight and to protect the glass from elbow and other risks. It slots into position on two large round-headed screws either side of the bottom sash. The top edge is not straight but is wavy or otherwise curved, and is usually brass mounted. Window boards are carved on the outside face, and stained and scroll-gilded on the inside.

IN-BUILT FURNITURE

The bed-place is two-berth and fills the whole width of the van at the end farthest from the door. The upper berth is about 6ft × 3ft 4in and the lower one somewhat narrower. In the Reading (Figs 15 and 16, see pages 150 and 151) the lower berth is rendered shorter than the upper one by the inward slope of the sides of the van, but it is quite large enough for children. Also in the three ledge-built types the lower berth is only 4ft 6in long, too small for any but a small child. In good weather it was customary only for children and elderly folk to sleep inside. The others liked to sleep on straw, heather or bracken in bender tents or under the waggon. They preferred the open air to comfortable beds.

In old waggons 18in from the sides are two floor-to-roof bed posts that are turned above the upper-berth level; below it they are square so that the doors that enclose the lower berth may be hinged to them. Instead of posts and doors, later vans save space by having sliding doors to the bottom berth. Where there are posts they run up to the arched roof-board, which is decorated with carving that often matches the outside crown-boards. Behind the upper berth and above the rear window a narrow shelf runs the width of the roof and usually has a spindle rail. In Bow-tops and Open-lots beds have no posts and pull out from single to double on wooden slide rails fixed to the sides.

Bow-top and Ledge waggons have three shallow drawers and a slide-in table top immediately below the upper berth, plus a deeper drawer on either side of the sliding doors to the lower berth. The Reading often has a larger pull-out table with fold-under legs.

Instead of bed posts and curtains, four sliding mirrored panels shut away the top berth in vans built after about 1905, excepting the Bow-top and Open-lot. The mirrors are bevelled, with a design cut into the silvered back surface. The two central panels are usually kept slid back behind the side panels to reveal the bed, the neatly curtained rear window and the china on the shelf above.

When there are no sliding shutters to the bed-place a board is slotted into position along the front of the berth, as in many ship's bunks, removable to enable the bed to be made. An earlier alternative is a fixed spindle rail.

The locker seat beside the chest of drawers and opposite the stove, and the second seat between stove and bed-partition, sometimes have tops that lift up and sometimes fixed tops with drawers beneath. They are either of french-polished mahogany or of pine stained, grained or scumbled. In good vans they are embellished with gilded scrolls, as are the other furniture and door panels.

The bow-fronted or bulge cupboard on the nearside corner as one enters has curved glass doors above and panelled door beneath. The one opposite is a wardrobe with panelled

BOW-TOP INTERIOR

Cross-section facing rear

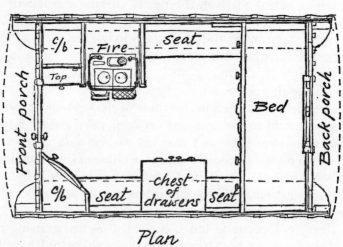

Plan

Fig 17

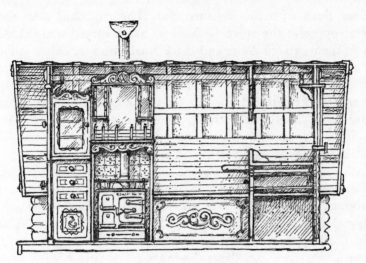

Section facing off side

Section facing near side

Fig 18

door flush with the fire-surround. The cupboard over the seat opposite the stove is shallow, has a carved and gilded pediment, glazed doors and three small drawers below it for cutlery. These have cut glass knobs matching those of the cupboard above. Other, larger drawers usually have brass tug handles. The glazed and mirrored, hinged cupboard doors are held closed with strong, brass latch handles, the best safeguards against their inadvertently swinging open— whether they are securely closed or not is fully visible.

Instead of the wardrobe of the Readings and Burtons, Bow-tops and Ledge waggons have a nest of small drawers above the ledge. They are knob-handled, have a shallow cupboard beneath and a recessed display cabinet above. Also in these types the chest of drawers has three drawers only, two short, one long, above the ledge level. Below it is a cupboard instead of the drawers of the non-ledge types.

That Gypsy caravans were built with secret hiding places for cash and jewellery is an old wives' tale. Glass-fronted cabinets or a drawer or two may have been built to lock, and occasionally a showman might have had a small iron safe bolted to the floor of a Burton, but that is all. Among Gypsies, vans change hands too frequently for secret places to remain secret for long. The Gypsy wife carries the *vongar*, money, with her, and gold or jewellery is worn.

SOFT FURNISHINGS

In the best waggons the bed was as sumptuous as it was possible to make it. Romany women took great pride in the quality and condition of their fine linen sheets and pillow cases, often bordered with hand-crocheted work or lace. Typically a bed would be furnished with a straw palliasse on the wooden slats forming its base, covered with a ticked mattress and bolster, feather- or down-filled, and white-linen-covered like the pillows. Over these would come a white linen sheet, Witney wool blanket, and white quilted and tasselled counter-pane. By the 1930s or thereabouts a spring mattress might be used and a satin-covered eiderdown. The patchwork quilt, by the way, is not characteristic. The high-born Romany woman took her cue, not from the cottager, but from the Victorian lady of the manor.

The upper berth is curtained when it does not have sliding shutters. The curtains are lace-edged or bobble-fringed, of velvet, silk or satin, and are tied back to the bed-posts with tasselled cord; they are essentially decorative, rarely untied.

Window curtains to this day are typically bobble-fringed or lace-edged, and looped back as drapes—as pretty as possible. Some vans have, as well as curtains, a spring roller blind with tassel and fringed bottom edge.

The back of the seat opposite the stove is often upholstered with buttoned-down leather-cloth, partly for comfort and partly to enable the shoulders of the person seated to clear the drawers of the cabinet above. There may also be, on this the most useful seat, a movable cushion matching the curtains. Another decorative touch is to the edge of all glazed cupboard shelves: they are trimmed with a bobble fringe held in place by brass-headed nails.

The floor, invariably covered with linoleum, is furnished with a skin rug or two, drugget or carpet. These, like the other soft furnishings, are of good quality in the best waggons, and some travellers dealt in such wares.

Peculiar to the interior of the Open-lot, and sometimes of earlier Bow-tops, is the additional storage for clothes and other things provided by an arras or screen of fabric matching the other soft furnishings, gathered on four flexible curtain-wires stretched along and against both sides of the bow.

161

FITTINGS

Apart from the brass rails and handles already mentioned, the fittings are for lighting, heating and cooking purposes. Normally cooking is not done in the van, however well equipped it may be for the purpose, but over the *yog* or wood fire outside, the stove being used only occasionally when weather or some other circumstance requires it, or for tea-making. (Incidentally, it is only of relatively recent years that the *gaujo*, with his charcoal grill and barbecue, has discovered a pleasure that the Gypsy has habitually enjoyed for centuries.) The stove, then, is used primarily for heating, and its quality and ornateness indicates family status, for the hearth is the heart of the home. The earlier stoves used in vans were open grates, later succeeded by enclosed ranges.

With the exception of the Burton, in which it is centrally placed between the two offside windows, the stove is approximately one-third of the way along the left as one enters, on the offside. Some vans in the nineteenth century were built with a 'Colchester' stove in the corner (Fig 2, page 33) immediately inside the door and, thus, it earned the soubriquet 'The Policeman in the Corner'; but the consequent uneven distribution of weight was found to cause buckling of the fore-carriage, particularly when the heavier range began to replace it.

The 'Colchester' was so-named after the town in which its suppliers, Beard and Son, established 1782, traded. An open grate cased in sheet iron, it has a brass front (kept polished like a mirror) and, to draw up the fire, a blower which slides down on brass side-rails. Below at floor level it has a rail guard, and above is a curved brass mantel shelf with rails, from which the conical top of the case tapers up to the roof to join the chimney. Some models have a side oven and trivet for a kettle. In 1915 the smallest 'Colchester' cost £7.25, the largest £8.75. The fire, not having an enclosing top, could burn various shapes and sizes of fuel, but its fault was that, when the van door opened, the ash blew everywhere.

This kind of stove continued to be used, especially in Bow-tops, but for many of the best equipped waggons by the early 1900s the 'Hostess' stove came to be preferred, made by Smith and Wellstood and sold through the ironmongers who catered for travellers (Fig 3, page 48). It is a cast-iron range with oven and closed top, having openings for carrying on several cooking operations at a time and plated rails to prevent pots from falling off. Beneath it is a sliding, brass-fronted coal-box.

In a van a closed range is normally boxed in with a carved and gilded wooden surround, and the recess so formed is lined with enamelled metal plates, floral or tile patterned. The top of the recess is a mantelpiece, with double or triple brass rail around it, 5-6in high. Above this is the overmantel, mirrored and with spindled shelves and carved pediment, masking the upper flue to the chimney above and the airing cupboard with its door at the side. On the mantelpiece would be displayed Staffordshire flatback figures and similar chimneypiece treasures.

Like the 'Colchester', the 'Hostess' came in various models and was catalogued as

> an admirably constructed stove for living vans, yachts, etc, having accommodation for every variety of cooking within the smallest compass, and with conspicuous economy of fuel. Splendidly finished with polished front mouldings and over-door mountings. A good sized oven for baking or roasting; hot closet underneath for warming plates; open front fire for toasting bread, etc.

In the 1880s the price of the smallest was £2.85, and £6.50 for the largest of six sizes. The plainest in 1956 cost £16.

Cheaper and smaller stoves were, of course, installed—the

'Skipper' for instance, 'for yachts and small coasting vessels, fishing and other boats, and for travelling or living vans'— but they are more utilitarian in appearance, and the 'Hostess' is the most typical of the best waggons. The name may be seen on the front of survivors together with a number which refers to size, not to pattern or date.

Another stove widely used is the 'Queen', colloquially 'Queenie', which combines ornateness, smallness of size (22in high by 16in wide) and cheapness. It is often used in today's Open-lots. In the 1880s it could be bought for ten shillings (50p). Its modern and plainer equivalent is about £12 and is even exported, to the United States for 'fun' use.

Other fireplace equipment comprises an iron or brass stove-lid lifter, a brass shovel, tongs and poker; and that for cooking includes a six or eight pint copper kettle with a well that fits into the stove-top opening, plus (though mainly for the outside wood fire) a large oval stew-pot and bucket-handled frying pan for suspension from the kettle prop.

Lighting after dark comes from a swivel bracket lamp screwed to the window jamb on the nearside between the locker seat and the chest of drawers. It is placed only exceptionally above the offside seat. Above it is a brass vent let through the roof to take away fumes and prevent sooting-up of the ceiling; beneath it, and as part of the fixture, is a reflector.

The quality of the bracket lamp, like that of the stove, signifies the degree of pride taken in the waggon as a home. The one most characteristic was called an 'Angel lamp' from the cherub embodied in its design, blowing like Pan on his pipes (see plate page 53, Fig 16). It is of brass and has a ruby-coloured cut glass fount, plated wick burner, chimney and hand-painted globe. The whole, complete, before 1914, cost around £2.50, today at secondhand perhaps six times that sum. Occasionally, these lighting fittings are nickel-plated to 'save work' but never look so well as when they match in with the warmth of the other brass and gilt in the van. Of course, they burn paraffin. Sometimes supplementary light is provided by candles in brass brackets fixed to the walls or bed posts.

Many travellers bought these and other fittings from the firm of R. H. Mellor and Sons, of Owl Lamp Works, Oldham, Lancashire, established in 1859 and 'manufacturers of every description of naphtha and paraffin lamps and burners, and all metal goods required by showmen.'

The general style of decor described in this chapter is of the 1900 period, when the Gypsy caravan reached its zenith. It has continued to be more or less typical of the best waggons built since.

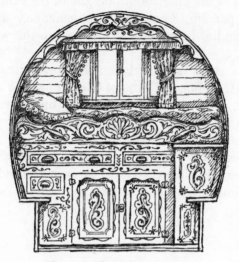

Cross-section facing rear

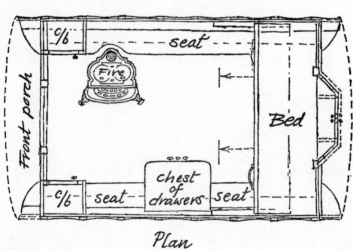

Plan

Fig 19

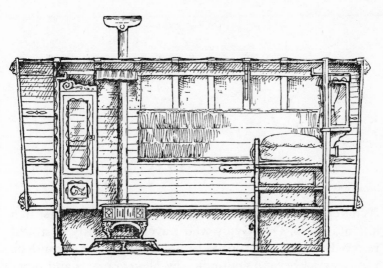

Section facing off side

Section facing near side

Fig 20

CHAPTER EIGHT

DECORATION

Its decoration is one of the first things to arouse interest in a fine old *vardo*. One Gypsy who travelled recently in a well restored waggon told us that he had had to sell it because he was pestered beyond endurance by photographers and other admirers who were as though magnetised by it. We suspect that there were other considerations too, but it could not have been easy for him to safeguard his family's privacy in a pristine home so colourfully redolent of the good life of the roads of seventy years ago.

The appearance of one other class of travelling habitation attracts similar attention, the narrow boat of the canals, with its Roses and Castles, scrolled lettering and ropework, and many people have speculated, not unreasonably, on some possible connection of origin. Both narrow boat and caravan are the homes of travelling people and are characteristically decorated; both were horse-drawn, the inmates of each swarthy lovers of bright colour. We ourselves once thought they might have a common denominator in the towns of the great horse fairs early in the last century—Northampton, Exeter, Nottingham, Horncastle, Howden, Woodbridge—all connected by waterways and some of them places where narrow boats were built. But most commercial centres are on rivers and, where not, became connected by canal. Also, although narrow boats date from the eighteenth century, it was not until around the passing of the Canal Boats Act in 1877 that they became decorated. Then the boatpeople, faced for the first time with having to keep their craft in good repair on pain of their boats (and therefore livelihood) failing to pass the statutory inspection, began to give them more attention and to embellish them. We believe that any resemblance between van and boat is superficial and may be put down to each taking its character from the taste of the same period and plebian class, reflecting the popular art of Victoria's time, still to be seen on old farm carts, pub architecture and furnishings, fairground rides, ship figure-heads and sternboards, toys and similar things.

One might play with the idea that among the foreign buyers who thronged the early Victorian horse fairs, or among the showfolk who came with circus or menagerie, there arrived some craftsman from, say, Hungary, who stayed here, found work with a waggon builder, and by his decorating ability gave his employer's vans something the others hadn't got, so influencing design in a direction that struck some chord in the traveller's memory. But it is not necessary to indulge fantasy to account for the waggons' 'foreign look'. Van dwellers as a class were cosmopolitan by descent, occupation and way of life. There certainly were craftsmen of foreign descent who worked on early vans, and in living memory, to our knowledge, German and especially Italian wood-carvers. Among the people who came to see one publicly preserved van in 1951 there was an old man who had been a craftsman in his youth, and he claimed to have carved its embellishments. He was a Sicilian. Anyway, unlike today, before 1900 there was no shortage of skill, native or immigrant, to provide show-folk, Romanies and others with the kind of decor that suited their taste.

The wheelwright and the fair-ground are in fact the main

sources of the kind of popular art with which we are concerned. *All* traditionally decorated *vardoes* are lined out—that is, embellished with lines of colour of varying thickness, emphasising the various forms. Lining-out occurs on the surfaces of English vehicles of many kinds, from coster barrow to coach, and was probably the outcome of the first attempt to emphasise the form of the wheel. It is traditionally English, and on Gypsy vans is used in an abundance probably greater than on anything else.

It was similarly natural for early van dwellers, closely related to the fair-ground in one way or another, to have their homes decorated in something of its style, increasingly baroque through the nineteenth century, a period when all decoration was extravagant. The travellers, conservative in everything, retained it despite the subsequent thinning out of decoration in other walks of life and its almost total abandonment in the 1920s.

CARVING

Carved or painted, the motifs are common to much Victorian decoration. Deriving mainly from Renaissance Italy, they were used not because of any symbolic meaning (despite well-spun Gypsy yarns) but simply because they were the wood-carver's and decorator's stock-in-trade. On vans they are perhaps more noticeable than on other objects because such work in abundance on simple vehicles was unusual in Britain. The amount of carving and the intricacy of paintwork were determined largely by the price the customer could afford, and it is likely that heavily ornamented vans did not pre-date the closing years of Victoria, though carving was used on vans dating from thirty or forty years earlier than that.

The earliest carving we have seen, in actuality and picture,

170

SOME CHARACTERISTIC WAGGON DOORS

Dunton

Tong

Wright (early)

Wright

Wright (late)

Hill

Fig 21

is on Readings, and Dunton seems to have set the pace for it. Not that the work of some other builders failed to match or even transcend Dunton's quality; only that he appears to have led the way at an early date. His porch brackets particularly were copied by others.

Although their productions varied according to buyers' needs, other makers especially noted for their carving were: George Orton, Sons and Spooner (whose Burtons for well-to-do showmen were superbly embellished), Wright, Hill, Tong, Howcroft, Watson (later Varney) and Jones (later Cox).

One principle is common to all good van carving: it is not merely rich but is always integrated, appearing to grow out of instead of being added to the structure. Good carving was rarely applied to ill-constructed vans, but it is not unknown for an otherwise good one to be spoilt by carving not designed for the position it was to occupy, causing it to look stuck on as a pretentious afterthought. Travellers themselves have occasionally 'had a go', inventing their own motifs and wielding the peg-knife with dash. But, however skilful the sculptor at subtracting wood from wood, the result, failing to grow out of the structure, is rarely more than quaint at best.

Unless (like Orton) they were primarily makers of fairground rides, thus having a large quantity of such work, few living van builders were themselves carvers or employed them whole time. Carving was normally 'bought' from a local or journeyman craftsman. For example, in the heyday of the *vardo*, Collier, the Leeds wood-carver, worked for various north-country builders. He did the carving on the Wright vans. Then for Herbert Varney, of Belper, Sid Burbeck did the work, plus a journeyman, Cyril Hookaby, 'in winters only'.

The waggon would be built, then pieces of wood would be cut to appropriate size, secured, then unscrewed, numbered and sent away to the carver with instructions. Usually he would be familiar with the builder's preferences, but sometimes supplementary specifications made by the client would require to be met from the carver's pattern book, or by copying the work of others, or even from verbal description. Sycamore, a home-grown timber, was mostly used, straight grained, fine textured and strong, and sometimes yellow pine of pattern-making quality. Dunton usually specified wych-elm for his porch brackets, easy to carve but unusually tough and split-roof, ideal for the job. Occasionally, mahogany was requested.

Apart from scrolls, curlicues, flowers, acanthus leaves, the grape-and-vine and similar stock-in-trade from the pattern book, the most frequently used motifs are almost inevitably hippic, especially for Gypsies—horses standing, walking, prancing, leaping, heads only, shoes, whips, wheels, etc. Among the features of the Bow-tops by Wright, Hill and other good builders are the running horse bounded with grapes-and-leaves filling the crown-boards over door and rear window, and the standing horse (with acanthus leaf filling the space behind the head) on the door panel—a popular successor to the earlier formalised sun-flower with spade-like leaves (Fig 21).

Taking the Reading as most typical, the centrepiece is the crown-board above the door (Fig 22). It usually bears either a carved or painted scroll. Carved ones like Dunton's were made in low relief from one piece of sycamore, and for extra depth of carving—for the central horsehead-shoe-and-whip motif—a piece was added proud of the wall line. Tong built several Readings for Gypsies which had alternative designs incorporating St George-killing-the-Dragon and Prince of Wales feathers.

A good Reading is nearly always distinguishable by its pierce-carved porch brackets (Fig 23), the front ones made

CROWN-BOARDS

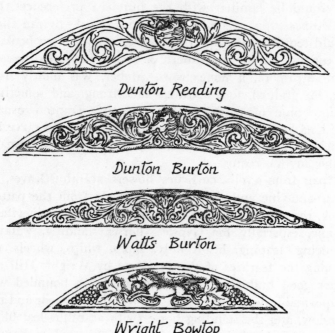

Dunton Reading

Dunton Burton

Watts Burton

Wright Bowtop

Fig 22

in one piece extending from eaves to footboard. Most early examples, and poorer vans of later vintage, have simple fretted brackets, but the earliest surviving Dunton brackets (c. 1890) are single, large, crudely carved acanthus leaves fanning out to eaves and footboard. By 1900 Dunton evolved an elaborately carved device comprising a generous volute surmounted by a scrolling acanthus, painted and 'flashed up' with gold leaf, enclosing a grapes-and-vine-leaf painted in natural colours. On later vans the central roundle or flower is surmounted by a gold bird like others on the door which, typically, contains three carved panels, two upright and one across the top. Dunton favoured a plain varnished mahogany door and front windows, the carving of scrolling, leaves and birds with grapes in their beaks being painted and picked out in gold.

An alternative bracket used by Dunton and others is an elaborate wheel-pattern. Wheel brackets of various kinds were often used. An old member of the Dixie family of Surrey Romanies called them 'noodle hops', but it seems to have been a term in family use only.

On the many variants of the Burton, porch brackets conform to no particular standard, but most of them have single, rather small though well-carved, brackets under the eaves fore and aft and none on the footboard. Burtons with double

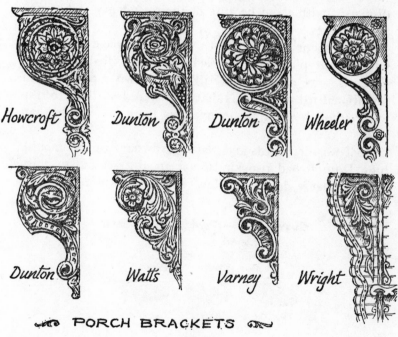

Howcroft   Dunton   Dunton   Wheeler

Dunton   Watts   Varney   Wright

PORCH BRACKETS

Fig 23

175

porch brackets in front, one above the other, typical of the Reading, are comparatively rare.

Between every rib at the bottom, middle and eaves many of the best waggons have small chip-carved brackets and mountings (Fig 12, page 134), but with these some travellers dispensed on the grounds that they increased the weight. For these and poorer travellers body carving was limited to corners and centres only.

On the arched weatherboards at each corner facing fore and aft are often carved lion-heads with a spout between their jaws leading from the gutters. The centre of each arched board bears another lion-head with mouth closed and having no function but decoration. Wright's early Ledge vans had three lion-heads on the side weatherboards but he later dispensed with them because of their tendency to be damaged by trees.

The butts or projections of the under-carriage are usually fiddle- or gryphon-headed (Fig 24). Some fiddle-heads scroll upwards, some downwards. Hill's were down, a practice that he rationalised on grounds that they were less likely to trap water (though there are many parts more susceptible than this).

Roof weatherboards and waistboards have carved mouldings. Dunton had two kinds: (a) an abstract design chip-carved—that is, done in shallow relief with a knife, an angled

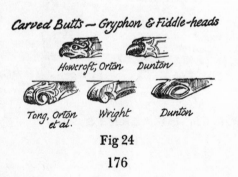

Carved Butts — Gryphon & Fiddle-heads

Howcroft, Orton   Dunton

Tong, Orton et al.   Wright   Dunton

Fig 24

flat chisel and a gouge; (b) a flower-and-crossed-ribbons motif also in low relief. Roof weatherboards of other vans often have a deeper moulding like an elaborate egg-and-dart. Those of Burtons tend to have straight moulding done with moulding planes. Some builders (for example, Howcroft), in place of weatherboards, had deep and elaborately carved cornices mitred at the edges around the van. They look decorative but heavy.

Howcroft's panelled waggons have four panels below the waistboard, sides and back, with carved bordering and a scrolled inset carving in shallow oak; these were screwed onto the pine panelling.

The side walls below the ledges of Ledge and Bow-top vans are usually of rib-and-panel construction, and these rectangular flat panels are of mahogany or red pine with a central scroll or floral device in gold with panel-lining an inch out from the frame and notched in at the corners. All the walls are embellished at corners and centre with inset carved pieces, like the Reading.

The relative cost of carving to the builder is a reflection both of monetary inflation and of the contraction in the numbers of craftsmen over half a century. After 1918 Dunton's standard grape motif porch brackets, so widely copied that two alike are not necessarily from the same hand, cost £5 the pair. Each of the two double porch brackets for the waggon front cost £5, and the singles for the rear £2.50 apiece: that is, £15 per van. Today one double bracket could cost up to about £50. In 1925 the cost of the carving for a Ledge waggon was about £25, including four lion-heads (5in × 4in) at £1.25. Today they would be about £5 each. Speaking generally the cost of carving on a well-built van represented about 15 per cent of the total.

PAINTWORK

Fifty or sixty years ago the painting represented about a quarter of an average total cost of £100 or £125. Today a re-paint may cost £500 or more (see Chapter Nine).

In the previous chapter we described the decoration of typical interiors, but here it needs to be added that the use of plain, household paint on woodwork, walls and ceilings, is entirely out of keeping. Cabinet work, when not of french-polished mahogany, is of pine, stained, grained or scumbled, with the carved and painted embellishments picked out in keeping with the colours and style of the exterior. Plain paint, flat or gloss, has no depth or richness, does not hide irregularities but emphasises them, and for this reason alone was not used by the old builders for interior work.

Also where a customer could not afford carving, painted motifs were often substituted, and it could be that carving of sorts appeared on waggons at an earlier date than paint, which may have found its way onto vans from the fair-ground. But, of course, by the time from which there are still surviving examples paint was used in its own right on both flat and carved surfaces.

Waggon painting is a skilled craft in itself that demands, in addition to mere know-how, practice over a long period in handling a range of brushes, in applying gold leaf, and in lining-out, cutting-in and shadowing. The work on the old waggons was done by specialist firms, by journeymen, or (most often) by individual members of the builder's family. Builders normally had, in all and including other vehicles, sufficient painting to do (unlike carving) to justify full-time occupation of at least one tradesman. Also, especially in later years, they re-decorated vans other than their own.

Again unlike carving, painting done by travellers themselves today often achieves the highest standards, even transcending the best of the old work. Open-lots, having little if any carving about them, provide plenty of opportunity for elaborate scrolling and lining (see plates pages 143 and 144); and museums and collectors have found that the best (and sometimes only) way to restore authentically is to use the services of painters of traveller stock (see Appendix). Of

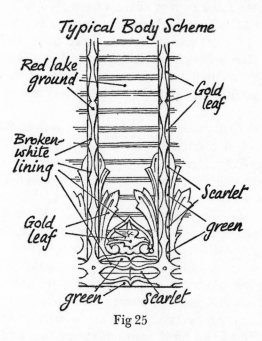

Fig 25

these Jim Berry, the Yorkshire Romany, is perhaps the best known. He can take up a sable writer and execute a freehand scroll down the S-curve of a pair of waggon steps with the ease and perfection of a calligrapher signing his name, but with one difference: he never repeats himself (see plate page 144). Such painters are often commissioned by travellers to 'personalise' their motor lorries and other vehicles by

179

decorating them in a modified style usually incorporating the Horse as the central motif.

Theory and practice were subject to experiment and change. Until World War II most builders made their own paint, buying the pigment in block, grinding it, and mixing it in turpentine with linseed oil. The amount of oil in each coat is critical, to avoid laying a 'lean' coat over a 'fat' one, which would cause crazing of the surface. To colour, bought ready-ground, a little gold size or varnish might be added to 'set' it, and further size or varnish added to the second coat. The chamfers were picked out, gold leaf applied, then the fine-lining, followed by one or more coats of varnish. All paint went on matt, gloss paint being a recent innovation still shunned.

The standard quality varied from firm to firm. Barnes and Son, the Belper coach and waggon painters who collaborated with the builder, Herbert Varney, used a coat of lead primer, an orange undercoat, then two coats of crimson lake with, finally, over chamfers, lining and gold leaf, a single varnish finishing coat. The semi-transparency of the crimson lake topcoat laid over the orange imparted a depth of hue unobtainable with opaque colour. Dunton, from our own observation in stripping down, used one coat of primer (red oxide for red lake vans, grey for green vans), followed by a single topcoat and one or two coats of varnish.

Varnishing was necessary both for protection and to provide a unified finish for the various matt paints and the gold leaf used. Gold leaf loses some of its pristine lustre when varnished, but if not so protected soon gets worn off exposed areas. Uncharacteristic of the *vardo* are the 'Flamboyant' colours used by the fairground painters—bright transparent enamels overlaying foil or aluminium paint to yield a metallic lustre. They look appropriate on rides, etc, but out of place on a living waggon. Traditional painters do not use them.

Colour schemes came and went as on vehicles for the gentry, and they had no particular mystique. We have found no evidence of any generally held belief that black was unlucky, as some Gypsy-lore writers have stated. As with motor-cars, when a van had a bad accident its colour might thereafter be held by the owner to be unlucky. Burtons and other showman's vans originally were painted predominantly yellow but later followed the Readings and Ledge waggons, which tended to crimson lake as a body ground with chamfers picked out in light red and gold, sometimes with green or blue, and lined in broken-white or straw. Some builders (for example, Jones and Cox) used red and blue for chamfers, restricting gold to the carving. Bright grass-green sometimes was chosen by Gypsies as a body colour for its landscape-blending quality (a desideratum not wholly aesthetic).

Apart from this one exception of grass-green, colour schemes were selected on aesthetic grounds solely, and sometimes appear to fly in the face of considerations of utility. For instance, underworks were almost always straw or pale yellow in colour, the wheels decorated with a broad red stripe on the sides of the spokes and fellie circle, sided by double fine-lining in light green. Chamfers on the underworks would be red, green and gold with gold flashing on the butts. Exceptionally, unders were painted bright red with green and gold chamfers and broken-white lining (Fig 26).

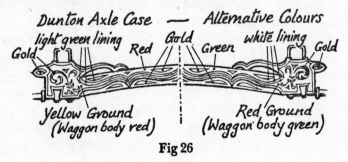

Fig 26

181

The carved porch brackets of grape-and-leaf design had a base of the body colour with lining, but the acanthus motif was gold shaded in with green or lake. The grapes-and-leaves were painted in natural colours. We have heard that Dunton used to put a bloom on the grapes as a finishing touch just before the waggon left the yard, dabbing them deftly with a little gold size and french chalk.

Windows were commonly either the body colour, one of the chamfer colours or, rarely, white. Dunton was likely to grain both frames and shutters, chamfered and lined over as the rest of the body. Shutters, and doors, ordinarily were the same as the body colour but, again, Dunton would often make doors of natural varnished mahogany, lined, with the carved panels picked out in colour and gold leaf. The underside of the porches was sometimes grained, matching the ceiling inside the van.

Originally chamfers were painted entire, using the flat of a fitch brush, one colour filling the whole chamfer and cut in with the lining. More recently this practice is often modified to painting an inset flash with a sable writer, revealing a border of the ground between it and the lined arris. This could have evolved as a kind of shorthand, or perhaps as a means of economising in gold.

According to their purse, most Gypsies insisted on gold, and for gold leaf there is no substitute. A gold paint has not been invented that out-of-doors doesn't tarnish to a dull brown within a few weeks. Gold leaf comes in two forms: transfer for flat areas, and loose leaf for carving. The part to be gilded is painted with gold size, usually with an undercolour of orange or red added, and when it becomes tacky or near-dry the transfer gold is pressed on. Loose leaf is worked into the detail with a soft brush. Use of loose leaf out-of-doors demands a calm day, for it crumples and blows away on the slightest breath of wind. A skilled craftsman under ideal conditions settled for almost thirty per cent wastage of gold leaf. French chalk applied from a pounce-bag before the gold size, prevents the gold sticking to the surrounding paint-work. In the early days of building, by some accounts, gold leaf was supplied between the leaves of a bible. When the 'books' came out in about 1920 they contained twenty leaves of 4in × 4in and cost 3s 6d (17½p). They are now over £1. The number of books used on a waggon has often been ex-aggerated, as many as 120 sometimes claimed, but forty books make an excellent job.

Templates were used for executing pictorial motifs like the running horse. They were fretted out of quarter-inch board, drawn around, painted or gilded out to the line and, when dry, were 'cut-in' or lined over the top. Also transfers depicting romantic themes with surrounding ornamental embellishment, sometimes backed with silver leaf for metallic effect, were used on some ceilings and cabinet-work panels. They were bought from an illustrated catalogue issued by the makers, J. H. Bulcher & Co Ltd, Moseley Road, Birmingham, who also supplied transfers for railway rolling stock and trams.

Lining, or lining-out as it is sometimes called, is a skill acquired through considerable experience backed by much practice. Conditions vital to good results are correct consist-ency of paint and a smooth surface over which to work it, but a steady hand is not essential. The long hairs of the lining brush, properly held, can take up the play of any but the shakiest hand. Confidence is essential and even the best hand with a liner likes a pint or two to prepare him for the work. The brushes (ox-hair liners) are in five main sizes identified by the names of birds, thus (from small to large): lark, crow, duck, goose and swan. Some painters cut down a lark to achieve an ultra-fine line for delicate work. In the old days feathers were sometimes used, and a piece cut from a bantam cock's tail would serve as a lark liner, though the bird-names probably have little significance.

The long hairs of the lining brush are bonded at the base by a short length of quill, which is held between thumb and forefinger. The hand may be steadied by resting the little finger on the work. The technique calls for a pot of flat colour, a pot of turpentine, and a pallet (which can be a piece of board or glass) on which to mix paint and turpentine to the right consistency. In executing a curlicue scroll, the painter holds the brush (a writer, like a long-haired watercolour brush) near the end of the handle and at right angles to the work surface; working from the thin to the thick end of a scrolling line, he makes the first stroke very freely, lightly sketched in, to be improved and thickened where necessary, with further strokes added.

From this elementary description it will be apparent that lining-out is a tricky business even for a fluent brush, but no waggon is its true self without plenty of it. Scrolls made with a stencil do not, of course, have the verve and vigour of those done freehand. Though it was usually carried out only on the square-panelled sides of Bow-tops, the *pièce-de-resistance* in the van decorator's art was scrolling and panel-lining in red or orange *between each rib* on a rib-and-matchboard van.

CHAPTER NINE

CONSERVATION AND COST

Urbanisation, the speed with which technology is changing every-day things, the growing rarity of obsolescent but pleasing objects used even within living memory, combine to encourage the interest in and appeal of old horse-drawn waggons and the kind of life that they represent, fancied or actual. The travellers themselves have gone over to the motor, some to modern Open-lots, and the few old *vardoes* still roadworthy appear only at horse fairs and other special events.

However, the desirability of the wandering life to the man or woman cooped up in factory, office or house is evidenced not only by motor-caravanning but by the horse-drawn kind of holiday. Where road conditions still exist that allow their pleasurable use, horse-drawn vans are still preferred by some, albeit a minority. These simple 'barrel-tops' are specially built for pleasure and are not classifiable within the compass of our subject, but they do merit mention. In Ireland and Wales at least roads still permit of horse-drawn caravanning on a substantial scale, and a good many people use the facilities of this kind that are offered there. The Irish Tourist Board found, for example, that in 1970, in the Republic, 13,300 visitors took their holidays in officially approved vans, and there were others there and elsewhere.

But the Gypsy caravan of yesterday is now a museum piece, sometimes well conserved but often in decline. Many have long since passed out of traveller ownership and into the possession of *gaujoes*. Wheels are made for turning, says the song, and a *vardo* in motion on the highway projects a gracefulness and character that, alas, are less apparent when it is at passive rest. Yet we prefer to see it well cared for, although in use for a purpose for which it was not intended, rather than in neglect and decay.

Outside of museums and folk collections, old waggons are in use for many purposes—to decorate the grounds of country hotels, restaurants, and pubs; as 'eye-catchers' in commercial trailer parks; as children's play-rooms, swimming pool changing rooms, retreats for writers and artists and others to whom privacy matters; and as holiday and other accommodation to supplement that of the owner's house. But they are not often treated with awareness of their growing rarity and, usually through ignorance, are not put into or kept in good condition. Even collectors and museums are sometimes at a loss to date and 'type' them correctly, and are unknowledgeable about them generally and their conservation.

DATING AND TYPING

Verbal statements regarding history of origin and ownership, unsupported by evidence, are usually not dependable or capable of confirmation. One example of provenance is of the Wright Ledge waggon in the Castle Museum, York. The axles, made by J. Woodhead and Sons, Leeds, bear their elephant-on-wall trademark, and are dated 1897, when the waggon was bought from Wright for £42.50 by Jacob Winter, whose wife was a Farrow. At Christmas of that year Isobel Farrow's son, Jacob, was born in it at Thornton-le-Dale, Yorkshire. It remained in the family until it came into the possession of Robert Dixon who let it out on a site at Tad-caster at 50p a week until World War II. Bob Farrow, horse-dealer of Ackworth, near Pontefract, bought it from him in 1941, washed it down, varnished it, and kept it for one month to attend a fair. He then sold it for £10 to Harry Robson, a farmer of Bishop Wilton, York, who painted it wartime green and used it, with wheels removed and stored, to house a farm labourer. In 1957 he sold it to the museum for what he had paid for it. In 1962 the museum had it repainted by Jim Berry for £150 (outside) and £35 (inside).

Vendors' claims regarding date of build are mere expressions of opinion unless authenticated (as above) by evidence capable of verification, and such opinion is often arrived at on superficial appearances only, which almost always suggest to the uninitiated that the age is greater than it is. 'Over 100 years old' and even 'Built about 1830' are not at all unusual claims, sometimes made in good faith; if true in fact, their soft-wood subjects must have been cossetted, unsubjected to hard wear on the roads.

The most reliable evidence is the maker's name and local-ity and the axle date. The name is usually cut in the face of the brass grease caps of the four hubs and is often obscured by layers of old paint. It is usually but not certainly that of the actual builder (the grease caps *might* have been taken from some other van). The date is usually incised by the axle maker on the axle-arms but is visible only when a wheel is removed. This date is not necessarily that of the van's build, as axles were sometimes renewed, but normally it is the most dependable indication of it in the absence of good evidence to the contrary.

Wheel removal (necessary also for greasing) requires care but is not difficult for anyone familiar with the same job on cars. Put the brake on hard and chock all wheels. Place a suitable jack under the axle close to the wheel to be removed;

*Adjustable
wheel spanner*

Fig 27

it must be firm and on a level plane. When the jack is raised and the wheel spins clear of the ground, apply a wheel spanner (Fig 27) to the grease cap and unscrew it anti-clockwise. One of two arrangements is then visible, though probably only after the surrounding greese has been wiped away: either two counter-threaded nuts or, more usually, a linch-pin and washer fixing. The first nut unscrews clockwise, the second anti-clockwise, and the wheel can then be slid off the axle spindle. Removing a linch-pin is rather more difficult but it can be shifted by levering up with a cold chisel or similarly shaped tool. Some wheels have a hole in the stock to facilitate this; if so, the wheel must be turned till the hole in the stock is uppermost, atop of the pin, which may then be pushed up and drawn out through it.

Other indications than axle date of period of build are approximate only, and it should always be kept in mind that travellers retained styles and manners long after they had disappeared from other walks of life. In Chapters 5-8 we have tried to show when various improvements and changes in design appear to have been introduced, and in dating these should be of help. Also our text, drawings and photographs should make it easy for anyone to categorise an old waggon, to 'type' it.

MAINTENANCE

It has sometimes been said that, if never overturned, a *vardo* will last about as long as a set of teeth. To this end it needs the same amount of attention for much the same reason. Maintenance—keeping it in condition, whether for the road or otherwise—today includes the following:

Providing permanent cover or at least screening from sunlight during the heat of the day in summer; hot sun devitalises paintwork more than any other weathering influence, and shrinks and cockles the timber, cracking the paint;

Standing the wheels on boards as protection against rising damp, even when stationary for a few days;

Turning the wheels from time to time;

Airing regularly by opening door and windows; keeping them closed causes deterioration that is rapid out-of-doors and unnecessary indoors;

Cleaning gutters and gargoyle water-spouts regularly of leaves and other debris;

Propping the shafts, or resting their tips on board or tile; stowing them away in a dry place protects them but spoils the appearance of the van;

Protecting the shafts, when off the road, by a piece of sheet over the framing, essential as strain sustained in travelling tends to open up the joints of the frame, allowing rain to penetrate;

Keeping all brass polished or lightly coated with grease so that it may be wiped off before polishing on special days; out-of-doors no lacquer treatment is effective for long, and only baking or stoving lacquer is durable indoors;

Washing down and varnishing during dry weather once

189

in two years, if permanently unprotected;

Greasing axles about once every month on the road, and oftener if they are not sound; neglect causes wear on the underside of the axle-arm and the inside of the box;

Packing grease-caps with grease;

Greasing ring-plates to ensure free turning of the lock; some have a small bridge on either side of the top ring for inserting the grease, and the plates of others can be wedged apart with a cold-chisel, the grease spread between;

Regular oiling of shackles and jackbolts on the suspension; those seized through disuse can usually be freed with penetrating oil, the operation afterwards aided by a heavy-weight person rocking the waggon from the inside;

Oiling springs regularly; their leaves should slide freely, one on another;

Oiling and greasing the screw-shank and bearings of the brake assembly, when on the road; though protected from weather beneath the body, they still need regular attention.

RENOVATION OR RESTORATION?

Renovation may be described as putting an old waggon into functional order, and this may be done to varying standards by wood-workers and decorators, where necessary with the assistance of specialist craftsmen like the wheelwright. But this is not restoration, which is a series of processes (including renovation) which seek to return the waggon to a state as near as possible to the original.

Invariably involved in renovation is the renewal of areas before repainting, the decay chiselled out and replaced with wood cut-to-size or with a resin filler, much as a dentist fills old teeth! Temporary preservation is possible by the liberal brushing of all woodwork with a colourless, dry-rot fluid. It has high penetrating qualities, restores the vitality of wood, and delays the rot process. It may be applied effectively over flaking paint but, as it will seal damp in, it is essential that the wood first be quite dry.

One cause of timber deterioration derives from the use of ferrous nails and screws by the builders, most of whom rarely used brass or copper fastenings. Rust can swell iron to about nine times its thickness, splitting the wood into which rain then soaks.

Rot usually starts at vital parts of the structure. The bottom sills or summers, for example, tend to trap moisture. Because of the ribbing on the outside, they are renewable only with difficulty, necessitating unbolting the body from the underworks.

The underworks do not often rot, being protected and of hardwood, but wheels do, usually at the point where the spokes join the fellies; and a set of new wheels for a Reading, say, could today cost £150, when obtainable.

Exposed to hot sun over long periods, the wooden parts of a wheel shrink, and the tyres, spokes and fellies loosen up as a consequence. To remedy this, Gypsies would roll their waggon into the shallows of a ford or pond to swell the wood, but the result is temporary only. One of the Kentish Smiths protected his wheels from the sun, and the brass frets from tarnishing, by covering the stocks when not on the road with four old felt hats. But serious loosening of the wheel structure is caused not so much through timber shrinkage as by the rolling out or stretching of the iron tyre caused by the continual pressuring and hammering on the road. The only corrective is to have the tyre off, shortened and shrunk on again, an operation known to the wheelwright as 'cutting and shutting'.

When axles have not been properly maintained, causing undue wear on axle-arm and box, wheels will not run well, a fault detectable by the play on the bearings. A wheel that

191

can be rocked back and forth more than half an inch or so when the rim is grasped at the top, has a worn bearing.

Once a spring has rusted badly the waggon will not run smoothly. The treatment is to take the unders apart, dismantle the spring assembly, clean up each individual leaf, lightly grease, then reassemble. All grease must be cleaned off exterior surfaces before painting. Springs and shackles that do not work freely put undue strain on the unders.

In replacing wooden parts it is essential to bear in mind that there may be apparently graceful curves in some members that originally were fashioned straight—bowing, for example, of the splinter bar and the back bars of the fore-carriage; these have been caused by stresses in the structure. Another related fault is the dishing in of the roof-line, when viewed from the side. It can occur in all types and may look attractive, especially in a Bow-top; but it is undesirable if only because with it goes an equal but ugly outward bulge to the van's sides. Whether it can be corrected depends on its extent, but it is a skilled job.

Old paint of course must be scraped or burnt off and the wood rubbed down before repainting, but the underside areas should be left unpainted, allowing the timber to 'breathe'. In redecorating the interior (as we have already indicated in Chapter Eight, plain paint should not be used except as a ground for decorated panels. The simplest treatment for pine cabinet work is: first a flat, rose-tinted stain (not varnish); then three coats of interior polyurethane varnish cut down with the finest steel wool; finally wax and polish.

Varnishing is essential both for protection and to unify the matt paints and the gold leaf used in the decoration. A good carriage or yacht varnish is necessary, but for the exterior the kind that is polyurethane-based is still suspect, it being considered perhaps too brittle for materials like wood that respond to changes of temperature and humidity.

When varnishing there must be no hint of humidity in the air or on the work. The right time is a warm sunny day in summer when the dew has dried off the grass. 'Start at twelve and finish at four,' is the old rule. Ignore it and the varnish may be quite matt the following morning or, even worse, carry a smokey bloom that obscures instead of pre-

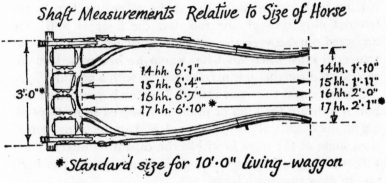

Shaft Measurements Relative to Size of Horse

14 hh. 6'·1"   14 hh. 1'·10"
15 hh. 6'·4"   15 hh. 1'·11"
16 hh. 6'·7"   16 hh. 2'·0"
17 hh. 6'·10" *   17 hh. 2'·1" *

3'·0"

* Standard size for 10'·0" living-waggon

Fig 28   *Often the first item for replacement*

serves the colours, an infuriating thing. Some claim that varnish bloom can be banished with a hot iron, but one traveller of our acquaintance, when the varnish bloomed all over a dray he had spent a week decorating, rid himself of it by taking a sledge hammer and smashing the thing up for firewood!

Roofs are best reproofed with heavyweight waterproof canvas, with an insulation of thin lining-felt beneath it, but it is an expert's job, and no nails may be used on the top surface of the roof. There is some advantage in painting a roof white or cream, as it then reflects sun heat to some extent and reduces the likelihood of blistering paintwork on the ceiling inside.

M

Waggon roofs were not designed to be walked over even where the ribs and longitudinal members appear to provide enough support. Too much weight on these may strain the side walls, which will then tend to bow outwards. Stepping on the roof at least demands laying down a plank first so as to distribute the weight. There are other hazards. One of the Lees was up on his roof one spring morning carrying out repairs. When finished he stood up to admire the view, lost balance and stepped into the middle of the mollicroft. He fell not only through the roof but the floor as well! He staggered out between the wheels laughing hysterically, and recovered only when his wife, whom he had passed on his way down through, hit him from behind with a pot-lid!

These remarks are not intended to teach van renovation but to indicate the kind of problem involved in it. Depending on the quality of result required, and on the initial condition, some of the work is within the capability of craftsmen without waggon experience, and perhaps enough has been said to show that some is not.

Restoration, which includes renovation, is a different matter. Waggons are often offered for sale as 'restored' when, at best, they are only renovated. Restoring—which, we repeat, means bringing the subject to a state as close as possible to the original—means working to the highest standards in various crafts and is impossible without expertise accumulated from long experience of various types and conditions of waggons, constructed at different times by different builders, and it demands the services of one of the few specialists in the work. The names and addresses of some of these are given in the Appendix.

It is for the owner, perhaps with expert advice, to make up his own mind as to whether restoration in the proper sense is worth while. Today it can cost up to £1,000 and more, depending on such considerations as whether the body requires to be removed from the unders, how much wood needs replacement, whether wheels need renewal, and so on.

VALUE, SALE AND PURCHASE

It may be appropriate to look at some prices of different types when they were new. A simple Reading built by Dunton with pine cabinet-work, no skylight and little gold leaf, cost about £70 in 1904. In 1913 a good one, completely fitted, was £125 to £150. In the 1930s it was not unusual for an old Reading in reasonable repair to be bought for £30 or £40, and a horse at about the same sum.

In 1910 the price of a new Ledge was from £30 for a plain one by a non-specialist maker to £125 for one of superlative build, complete with fittings. The latter, new in 1925, would have cost £175, and in the 1930s £200-£300. In 1910 Wright's lowest price Ledge was £73 'with no gilt...you find your own lamps, etc'.

A Bow-top by Wright in 1910 cost £68 'with furniture and gilded carved work' but again 'you find your own lamps.' In about 1930 Hill charged £120 for a Bow-top with gold leaf.

Just before World War 1 a good Burton cost from £100 to £150, about the same as a Reading; and by the 1940s, if still sound, the same waggon could have fetched £200.

In 1971 the price of an Open-lot, new, might be from £350 to £700, and an excellent one built in the summer of 1969 for Fred Walker, the Romany, cost £800, he supplying the dray on which it was built; of this, over half was for the painting by Jim Berry. It changed hands several times in its first year, most recently for a reputed £1,400.

The prices quoted are those paid by travellers. Theoretically, a waggon bought for the use for which it was originally intended is worth more than it otherwise would be but, offsetting this, a *gaujo* is usually expected to be willing to afford more than a traveller, whatever his purpose. Some auctioneers say that owners often have inflated ideas of value, and do not make allowances for the relatively limited market for an object of such size, no longer required for its original purpose. To be shown as it should be it needs a sizeable piece of ground, ideally under cover, temporary or permanent; it needs maintenance attention; and the cost of restoration may be as much as or considerably more than the cost of the van itself. These considerations all limit the market, yet museums, collectors, decorators, country-lovers and others, including well-to-do visitors from overseas, are always on the lookout for good examples, and the seller's problem is to establish contact with them.

Old waggons are advertised for sale in *The Times*, *The Sunday Times*, *The Observer*, *Country Life*, *The Field*, antique periodicals and other publications. They come up from time to time at auction sales, and sometimes are on offer by country antique dealers with large grounds to their premises. And, of course, they are bought and sold by travellers themselves, usually at horse fairs like Appleby in Westmoreland. Where a wheelwright can be found through the classified pages of the telephone directory, he is often a source of information.

Values vary at least as much as condition, the asking prices noted in the last year or two being as low as £50 ('needs restoration') and as high as £2,500 ('antique Gypsy Queen's, with original brass, carving, stove, etc'). In 1970 Swettenham, Whitehouse & Co, Chester, sold at auction for £1,000 a late nineteenth century Reading ('restored by a vicar and used by him as a country retreat'). Wentworth Auction Galleries, Virginia Water, Surrey, in the same year sold a good Burton ('for a swimming pool') at £460. In 1971 at King & Chasmore's Pulborough salerooms, Sussex, a good Bow-top fetched £680, a Reading of poor condition but original finish went

196

for £400 and another re-finished and repainted for £320.

Thimbleby & Shorland, who have held monthly horse sales at Reading for seventy years, conduct two collective sales annually of driving vehicles and carriages, and prices realised there have included the following:

Bow-top restored to 'as new' condition, fully fitted: £415.

Burton by the Hartlepool Carriage Co, requiring repainting £100 (a low reserve).

Bow-top repainted and gold-leafed, original fittings: £605.

Miniature Gypsy van craftsman-built as a show-piece to suit a 12hh horse: £285.

Miniature Reading in show condition for Shetland pony: £150.

These examples are general indicators only without more details than it is possible to give here. The highest price of which we have knowledge is £9,000, paid by a Swiss buyer, but it was for an exceptional, coach-built masterpiece kept in store from the day it was finished for reasons equally exceptional. Outside of a small circle of specialists, considerations that should influence values—true condition and its closeness to original, whether and how well renovated or restored, builder's reputation, date—do not always do so; and price is as likely to turn on luck and bargaining as on anything.

Among travellers themselves a *vardo* often changes hands not for cash but by 'doing a chop', perhaps with a bit of *vongar* thrown in to redress any balance. Argument *in extremis* is involved, but when agreement is finally reached the buyer ratifies it by slapping the seller's out-stretched palm, the travellers' equivalent of completing the contract. Dealing is a game as much for its own sake as for considerations of need. A Gypsy seldom rejects the chance of a good *chop*. In 'chopping the waggon away' it's the woman who suffers, yet in practice she often reacts philosophically to upheavals of the kind. It is customary to leave the window curtains behind as a gesture of goodwill towards the buyer.

What to look for when inspecting should be evident from what has already been said, but we repeat that of prime importance is the condition of the undercarriage and wheels. Woodwork can best be tested with the point of a knife, not always injected with the owner's knowledge, for it's the surface of the timber that is last to decay. When new, paint can hide serious trouble, and pockets of rot that actually reach the surface can be readily disguised with putty before repainting. But the discerning eye can detect them, and any irregularity of surface warrants suspicion and investigation.

Back in 'waggon time', when to Gypsies van-living and van-dealing were almost synonymous, a traveller interested in a waggon might contrive to visit the owner after dark. Any cracks and holes in the structure, hard to detect by day, made a merry display at night when the lamp was lit in the van.

APPENDIX

**Public Collections
with Examples**
City Museum, Queen's Road, Bristol 8.
County Borough Museum, Reading, Berkshire.
Folk Museum of Yorkshire Life, Castle Museum, York.
Mary Arden House, Wilmcote, Stratford on-Avon, War-
    wickshire.
Welsh Folk Museum, St Fagan's Castle (National Museum
    of Wales) near Cardiff.
Worcestershire County Museum, Hartlebury Castle,
    Hartlebury, near Kidderminster.

Some Restorers & Decorators
*Joe Barras, Thinford House, Thinford, Co. Durham.
*Jim Berry, Yorkshire (no fixed address, location obtainable
    only on enquiry of other travellers).
*Tom Clarke, Lyndhurst, Buxton Road, Chinley, Cheshire.
*Charles & Bob Farrow, Ackworth, near Pontefract, York-
    shire.
*Tommie Gaskin, Tilts Lane, Tollbar, Doncaster, Yorkshire.
**Denis Harvey, 22 Rose Hill, Dorking, Surrey.
*Peter Ingram, c/o Worcestershire County Museum,
    Hartlebury Castle, Hartlebury, near Kidderminster.
*Mervyn Jones, Downing Cottage, Holywell, Flintshire.

John Pockett, Pockett's Yard, High Street, Cookham, Berkshire.

J. Williams, Tadley, near Aldermaston, Berkshire.

*Occasionally build Open-lots.
**also Wood-carver.

Architectural Ironmongers
Cluse, Ltd, 5 Percy Street, London, W1.

Victorian Oil Lamps
Christopher Wray's Lighting Emporium, 600 King's Road, London, SW6.

Robert Eldridge, Redcliffe Square, Kensington, London, SW10.

Stoves
Smith & Wellstood (Mfg) Ltd, Columbian Works, Bonnybridge, Scotland, & 2-16 Goodge Street, London, W1.

Advertisements for and of Vans & Equipment
Exchange & Mart, 10-12 South Crescent, Store Street, London, WC1.

The World's Fair (showman's weekly), Union Street, Oldham, Lancashire.

Wheelwrights, Carvers, etc, see classified pages of telephone directories.

BIBLIOGRAPHY

Gypsy Caravans

Harvey, D. E. 'English Gypsy Wagons', 2-page illustrated article in *Architectural Review*, May 1951

Harvey, E. 'English Gypsy Caravan Decoration', 11-page illustrated article on Gypsy carving in the *Journal* of the Gypsy Lore Society, Vol 17 1938

Huth, F. G. 'Gypsy Caravans', 40-page illustrated article in the *Journal* of the Gypsy Lore Society, with introduction by E. O. Winstedt, Vol 19 No 4 October 1940

Monteith, M. 'Gypsy Caravans', 6-page colour-illustrated article in *The Field*, November 17 1966

O'Driscoll, F. 'Painted Wagons', illustrated article in *The Lady*, March 20 1969

Smith, D. 'Gypsy Caravan Painters', 10-page illustrated article on Gypsy painters in the *Journal* of the Gypsy Lore Society Vol 48 1969

Gypsies & Other Travellers

Borrow, G. *Lavengro* 1851
    The Romany Rye 1857
    Wild Wales 1862
    Romano Lavo-Lil 1874
Boswell, S. G. *The Book of Boswell* 1970 (autobiography)

Dodds, N. *Gypsies, Didikois & Other Travellers* 1966 (travellers today)

Hoyland, J. *A Historical Survey of the Gipsies* York 1816

McEvoy, P. *The Gorse & The Briar* 1938 (autobiography)

Mann, S. E. 'Gypsies', article in *Encyclopaedia Britannica* 1959

Department of the Environment. *Gypsies & Other Travellers,* HMSO 1967 (only official publication, a study by Ministry's sociological research section)

Phillpotts, E. *The Broom Squires* 1932 (brush makers, fiction)

Reeve, D. *Smoke in the Lanes* 1958
       No Place Like Home 1960
       Whichever Way We Turn 1964
(all three describe waggon life on the road by a traveller)

Simson, W. *A History of the Gipsies* 1865

Smith, R. *Gipsy Smith—His Life & Work by Himself* 1904 (Gypsy evangelist's autobiography)

Gould, S. B. *The Broom Squire* 1896 (brush makers, fiction)

Vesey-Fitzgerald, B. *The Gypsies of Britain* 1944/6 (includes a chapter on waggons)

Travelling Showmen

Bostock, E. H. *Menageries, Circuses & Theatres* 1927

Braithwaite, D. *Fairground Architecture* 1968

Dickens, C. *The Old Curiosity Shop* 1840 (Mrs Jarley's caravan)

Disher, M. W. *The Greatest Show on Earth* 1937

Murphy, T. *History of the Showmen's Guild 1889-1948* Oldham *circa* 1949

'Evolution of Amusement Machines', lecture, *Journal* of the Royal Society of Arts, September 7 1951

Sanger, G. *Seventy Years a Showman* 1926

Tyrwhitt-Drake, Sir G. *The English Circus & Fair Ground* 1946

Horse & Highway

Arnold, J. *The Farm Waggons of England & Wales* 1969

Jenkins, J. G. *The English Farm Wagon* Reading 1961 (reprinted by David & Charles 1972)

Margetson, S. *Journey by Stages* 1967 (road travel to 1840)

Ministry (& Board) of Agriculture. *Annual Reports*, statistics regarding horses

Sturt, G. *The Wheelwright's Shop* Cambridge 1923

Vesey-Fitzgerald, B. *The Book of the Horse* 1946 (with a chapter on The Horse in Trade)

Recreational Caravanning—Historical

Stables, W. G. *Cruise of the Land Yacht 'Wanderer'* (first book on recreational caravanning)

Stone, J. H. *Caravanning and Camping Out* 1912

Whiteman, W. M. 'The Caravan & Its Impact on Society', lecture, *Journal* of the Royal Society of Arts, January 30 1957

*Place of publication is London unless
stated otherwise*

ACKNOWLEDGEMENTS

No book of this kind is possible without the willingness of many people to provide information, guidance and other assistance on aspects of the subject with which they are familiar, and our thanks are due for so many kindnesses that it is hardly possible to acknowledge them all.

However, of particular importance were the active co-operation and advice of Mr Ferdinand Gerard Huth, a Gypsyologist who studied living waggons for many years before publishing in the *Journal* of the Gypsy Lore Society in October 1940 the results of his basic work, describing in technical detail the characteristics, design, construction and decoration of various types of van, their equipment and harness, as he had known them. Had he not done so our task would have been much more difficult.

Especially helpful, too, was the assistance so readily given of Mr John Pockett, one of the very few whole-time restorers of horse-drawn waggons, Mr Tom Clarke, a wheelwright as well as a restorer, and Mr Mervyn Jones of Holywell, Flintshire. Other restorers to whom we are grateful are Mr Peter Ingram and Mr J. Partington-Smith.

Where we could find them, the few builders who have survived from 'waggon time' and the descendants of others once engaged in the crafts involved, were invariably most willing to provide such facts and memories as they could muster. For help of this kind we are notably indebted to Mrs E. Miller and her daughter, to Mrs Bessie Dunton, to Mr Rowland Hill and his son, to Mr George Cox and to Mr Thomas Tong.

The co-operation of museum officials was most valuable, and we especially acknowledge that received from Messrs T. L. Gwatkin (Reading County Borough Museum), Andrew Jewell (Museum of English Rural Life, University of Reading), R. Patterson (Castle Museum, York), and N. Eric Wilkins (Mary Arden House, Stratford-on-Avon).

We also thank, among the many travellers, craftsmen, collectors and others who have assisted us, Messrs N. E. Arrowsmith-Browne, H. Vernon Barnes and Bill Watson of Belper, Sylvester Gordon Boswell, A. Estler, Eric Goodey, C. B. Goulandris, G. V. Hinde, King and Chasemore of Pulborough, John Mauger (of Thimbleby and Shorland of Reading), R. Plewes, Brian Raywid, David Smith, Henry Smith, Brian Thompson, Richard Wade, Fred Walker, David Weekes, J. Williams (Tadley), and also Mrs Jackie Bradfield, Mrs Rita Harvey and Miss Dora Yates (Honorary Secretary and Editor, Gypsy Lore Society, University Library, Liverpool).

C. H. Ward-Jackson
Denis E. Harvey

Polruan, Cornwall
& Dorking, Surrey

205

Horse-drawn living wagons have been used by gypsies in England for at least 150 years, and the best were built in the Victorian era, notably in the last quarter of the nineteenth century. The people of the roads called their wagons their homes, or *vardos*, but townspeople called these vehicles gypsy caravans. To the gypsy, his *vardo* was his most valued possession. Distinctive, functional and handsome, it would be hard to find a better symbol of the traveling people. Few gypsies currently live in caravans, and many of the wagons are now museum pieces. However, it is still possible to buy a new caravan, or to restore an older one.

In this book, the caravan's characteristics are defined, and the authors outline its history and technology, recall its builders and describe the six main types—their decoration, construction, furnishing and conservation. There is a fine collection of photographs and drawings (including the first scale drawings made of existing types of wagons) which make this book the definitive work on its subject.

211

INDEX

Illustration pages are indicated by italics

207